Intermodal Shipping Container Small Steel Buildings

Second Edition

By Paul Sawyers

This publication describes the general procedures for building structures out of shipping containers. The process of building anything depends largely upon the skill of the builder, the materials used, the machinery employed, and the conditions under which the work is performed. The author cannot and will not assume any liability for damage to persons or property or other consequences of any procedures or designs referred to herein or of any omissions relating to techniques, design, materials or procedures. Construction of container buildings is regulated by your local municipalities building department. Fee's, permits, and design approvals are assumed to be a prerequisite of construction. The author makes no claim of ownership or novel invention regarding the construction methods shown or the designs presented in this publication.

Published by Paul Sawyers
www.paulsawyers.com

Contents

Preface

The history of cargo ships and long distance trade between peoples dates back thousands of years. Long before the current handful of economic systems now in place, mankind was exchanging goods by way of simple straight forward trades.

Sailors set out to sea in vessels of wood and rope hauling precious domestic cargos later returning with exotic imported goods. The world was unending back then, and full of mysteries, but in the past 100 years, the world, or global community as we now call it, has been shrinking. It can be seen in the rapid satellite news coverage from far corners of the globe, a non-stop flight from Seattle to Hong Kong, or on a container ship as it powers through the open Pacific.

There have been extreme advances in geographical knowledge and ship technology, and many aspects of international trade itself have changed since the old days.

This is a book about small steel buildings, true, but it's difficult to make commentaries on the current state of global trade when the main subject of this book (containers) plays such a major role in the theme.

China manufactures and exports just about every kind of item you imagine. The United States takes in these goods at an astonishing rate, but it exports very little back to China.

The United States is an example of a country with surplus empty shipping containers. They gather near intermodal ports and rail hubs.

The worlds largest manufacturer of intermodal shipping containers is a South Korean Corporation called Jindo. If you purchase a shipping container today the chances are high that it was built by Jindo.

With higher labor costs in Korea, and increased Chinese competition, Jindo recently took the drastic step of closing its South Korean operations and moving all manufacturing to China. This example shows how global trade effects not only what is shipped inside containers but the very containers themselves.

The future will be interesting to say the least because, yes, our planet is shrinking and this shrinking is increasing at an unquestionable rate.

Once major shifts in global economics have been set in motion it's difficult to slow the momentum.

Shipping container structures will help to provide housing and shelters in this rapidly changing world.

I can think of no other building material that could possibly offer more solutions to problems perhaps caused by it's own propagation.

Introduction

This book is designed to guide you through the process of setting up a small building comprised of steel shipping containers. The buildings range from 160 square feet to 960 square feet with additional mid-span square footage provided on some designs. The shipping container which takes on the form of a utility structure has many applications. Fabricators, artists, builders, welders, hobbyists, agriculture, and so forth.

Container structures can be built with wide mid-span roofs, or by setting several units side-by-side to create buildings wider than what you might normally envision when you think of a shipping container. The eight foot width is the standard starting point but it's usually added on to. Containers are essentially giant building blocks that you can arrange to create larger structures.

You might have an existing wealth of knowledge regarding this subject or none at all, or have some limited idea of the concept. Both experienced builders and novices have been making use of this simple, strong, secure almost instant structural component (iso containers) at an ever increasing rate, but container structures have been around since at least the 1980's. Movie goers viewed an elaborate set consisting of container homes and structures built in the 1985 science fiction film 'Space Rage: Breakout on Prison Planet'.

There are many ways to put a container building together. Container buildings can be a gritty single twenty foot unit with a workbench inside, or a clean stripped-down modernistic design. The natural problem solving skills of builders or potential builders tend to thrive when planning structures using the standardized dimensions of containers available.

7

You may be searching for a vision of a building or have one all planned out in mind, but generating a vision perhaps during the course of reading this book is extremely helpful. Vision provides motivation to move forward with your chosen design and often solves construction issues ahead of actually encountering them.

The plans and information contained here are geared towards the individual builder working on a budget. In a nutshell, this book will strive to provide the bulk of it's content in the following two areas:

1) Plans for constructing three different super strong steel buildings under 1000 square feet in size.

2) Plans for foundations, roofs, framing, movement, and other universal aspects of container building that are interchangeable on these and other small scale container building projects.

1. Intermodal Containers: Building Blocks

Today, ocean going cargo is shipped in steel boxes called Intermodal containers. Intermodal shipping containers are heavy duty welded steel boxes designed and manufactured to transport goods safely over the high seas, but they also present a low cost, easy to construct, and super strong building solution. These boxes are built to strict international quality standards, to survive harsh treatment and a violent life in the marine environment. They are known as cargo containers, shipping containers, sea boxes, or ISO containers (International Organization for Standardization).

Shipping containers can be looked at as simple building blocks. Placement of containers side-by-side (in a permanent building form) will create an interior space comparable to many small building designs. One single 20 ft x 8 ft container will make a nice small workshop or utility building. You will see that foundations are not necessarily required (as discussed in chapter 3), but you should use some type of footings. Two joined 40 ft containers, resting on concrete footings, and topped with a lumber-built gable style roof creates an affordable useful structure that is really quite easy to build.

The simplicity of construction speeds the building process considerably. If you know you can construct a building, but become overwhelmed with all the details, materials, sources, time frame, etc, container building might help. The lack of materials required can ease one's mind considerably. You really only need one or two containers, and some form of footings ... that's it. If you want, additional structural aspects can be added at your leisure or when funds dictate. Add a gable roof, wiring, extra doors and windows, even interior walls. One days worth of critical coordinating can be expected on delivery day, as you will be dealing with the trucks, and perhaps rental of a small truck mounted boom crane (if needed).

Containers can also be used in conjunction with a factory steel, or lumber built structure, as an extension of the building. If for example, you want a permanent storage room attached to the building, a container installed in that area could do a nice job with little effort.

If you are building a traditional lumber structure, a container can be used as temporary housing and secure tool storage on site, then permanently installed as a workshop when your lumber structure is completed, or you can sell it.

Shipping containers are often thought of as the big steel cargo boxes that spend most of their service life on ships. In reality many shipping containers spend more time on land (in port and on rail) than afloat.

The sea voyage can be the shortest leg of the journey once a container makes it's way far inland in an import heavy nation such as the United States. Simple economics comes into play at the point where an empty container in Chicago could be sold to a container reseller vs being hauled back to a coastal port via rail in it's empty state.

The term Intermodal refers to a containers ability to be loaded onto ship, rail, or truck with a special stackable chassis. It is Inter-Modal, meaning the cargo stays in the box as it traverses from land to sea, back to land, and finally to it's destination. The box goes from one "mode" of transport to another with ease.

Containers are adaptive by design and possess the natural qualities of a small land based structure. The three methods of container transport are ship, rail, and truck.

The freight industry measures container shipments as TEU's. One 20 ft container equals one TEU, one 40 ft container equals two TEU's. The global economic growth experienced during the 1990's resulted in the manufacture and deployment of more TEU's than ever before. It is uncertain if these trends will continue.

Fuel can increase or decrease in cost, countries that import may experience economic recession, countries that export may experience political upheaval, and so forth. The factors effecting trade are numerous and too varied to hazard a guess at what might alter shipping container distribution trends. Nevertheless, many containers are already stockpiled within import-rich countries. Excess containers are a good thing for the budget minded Intermodal builder because large supplies usually indicate an open availability for the general public to purchase at fair prices.

This book, as discussed in the introduction, will provide an assortment of building designs made from these containers, but before we get into that, let's take a brief look at the history of the cargo container.

Brief History of The Intermodal Container

Containerization introduced pre-packed boxes loaded by crane that displaced large numbers of dock workers and made a once common occupation much less so; Longshoreman. The old way of loading cargo on ships was slow, and there was a high incidence of damaged goods. Cargo had to be packed in wood crates for shipment. Longshoremen then moved these crates around the docks, and guided them as cranes lowered the goods into ships cargo holds.

The Intermodal system streamlined this process but took time to catch-on due mainly to the large infrastructure of dock systems and cranes required at each port. These (usually rail-mounted gantry type cranes) had to be built at the wharfs to load and unload container vessels. Smaller cranes and forklifts were also needed to move containers on and off trucks, not to mention the specialized truck chassis and rail flatcars needed for inland transport.

Container Innovation Timeline

1926 - Thoburn and William Brown (Brown Industries of Spokane WA) began experimenting with lightweight aluminum trailer bodies. In addition to building the first all-aluminum airplane, and the first all-aluminum bus with rear engine, Brown Industries is credited with building the first shipping containers for use on trains and ships.

1934 - Trucking entrepreneur Harry Werner purchased the rights to Brown's development.

1939 - Harry Werner joined with associate Joe Numero. They enlisted the help of inventor Fredrick Jones to solve the problem of transporting cold cargo across the country. This leads to creation of The Thermo King, the worlds first refrigerated container.

1940-45 - Werner worked with the U.S. Army to create a standardized 8 foot steel container that could be pre-loaded before placement on ships for transport to Europe. This box could then be lifted onto trucks, and transported directly to theaters of war as required.

1949 - Werner is contacted by the shipping company Ocean Van Lines (OVL) with the first order for commercial containers. OVL had just landed a government contract to transport military supplies from Seattle to Alaska (to fortify the Aleutian Islands as the cold war escaladed).

1950 - Werner sold only a few hundred containers to the U.S. Military during the first half of the 1950's. Despite a large advertising campaign in the Nations largest newspapers, buyers failed to appear. Many small and medium sized companies realize the benefits, but lack the funds to build specialized docks, truck chassis and cranes for handling containers.

1955 - Trucking giant Malcolm McLean studied the problems and made plans for his own fleet of container ships. In 1955 he sells his trucking company for six million dollars and uses these funds to form a new company called Sea-Land, dedicated to the development of containerization.

1956 - Sea-Land launched the worlds first commercial container ship, the Ideal X. It services ports up and down the east coast. The shipping industry takes note, and container use begins to catch on.

1966 - McLeans Sea-Land launches the first transatlantic shipment of containers.

1970 - Container design is standardized world wide with the introduction of ISO 668.

The International Organization for Standardization (ISO) shipping container standards are the blueprints that all nations must follow in regard to construction and use of containers.

ISO 668 - Series 1 freight containers - Classification external dimensions and ratings [Amd 1993]

ISO 830 - Terminology in relation to freight container [Amd 1988]
ISO 1161 - Series 1 freight containers - Corner fittings Specification [Amd 1990]
ISO 1496-1 - Series 1 freight containers - Specification and testing [Amd 1998]

ISO 1894 - General purpose series 1 freight containers - Minimum internal dimensions [2nd 1979]

ISO 6346 - Freight containers - coding, identification and marking - [1995]

The hurdles of modern shipping have spawned many variations of containers. These categories include; open top, platform, tank, reefer, and air/surface containers to name a few. The main category of container remains general purpose containers, yet subcategories within the general purpose models are varied. These variations include; high cube, double end doors, side wall doors, open sides, and so forth. The most common containers are steel 20 and 40 foot general purpose containers. These are also commonly referred to as dry cargo containers or box containers. They are 8 ft wide and 8.5 ft high universally except for high cube models that are 9.5 ft high. These basic steel containers make up an estimated 80% of all containers in use worldwide. These are the type of containers I will refer to throughout the book.

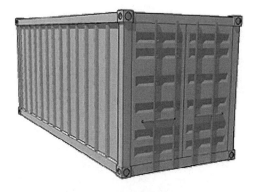

Steel containers are constructed of 14 gauge (.075") corrugated sheet steel panels that are welded to the main structural 7 gauge (.18") tubular steel top and bottom side rails and end frames. These end frames are fitted with ISO standardized cast steel corner fittings at all eight corners. These are welded to four corner posts, top and bottom side and front rails, and rear door sill and header. These corner fittings are what holds a container together. The roof is constructed of corrugated sheet steel panels welded to the top side and end rails and door header and may have roof bows for support. The doors are steel panels fitted with locking and anti-rack hardware and weather-proof gaskets.

The steel used to build modern containers is usually corten steel. It's a corrosive resistant high-strength low-alloy steel that conforms to the Japanese Industrial Standard G3125.

The main structural components of a shipping container are; corner fittings, corner posts, bottom side rails, top side rails, bottom end rail & door sill, front top end rail & door header, plywood floor, front end wall, bottom cross members, roof panel, side panels, and the doors.

The side walls of containers are comprised of large one piece sheets of corrugated corten steel. The pattern (number of corrugations) varies widely on similar size containers. Corrugation patterns provide vertical strength along the sides of the container.

Many container structures feature large portions of removed side wall material or complete removal of a full side wall. This is a popular method of increasing the interior width of a container building.

Side wall removal will result in a loss of rigidity equivalent to the amount of material removed. Full side wall removal will result in a most noticeable floor flex. Containers modified in this manner should receive at least two mid-span braces on a 40 ft container and one brace on a 20 ft model.

This will protect against expected flexing of the top and bottom side rails. It's also important to install a footing under each brace to transfer vertical stresses into the ground. See Chapter 6 Fitting Out Container Buildings for more on side wall removal and bracing.

The roof of a shipping container is constructed with several (5 per 20 ft, 11 per 40 ft) die-stamp corrugated steel sheets with a certain upwards camber at the center of each trough and corrugation. The camber provides a mild doming of these roof panels to promote water run-off. These sheets are butt jointed together to form one panel by automatic welding. The roofs main purpose is to keep out the elements. It is not a load bearing component, yet is capable of supporting a 440 lbs evenly distributed load (limited to a single 6 sq foot area at one time - like two people walking over it) without damage.

The bottom of general purpose shipping containers can vary in several ways based on the design pattern of 3-4 mm thick cross members. 20 ft containers may have forklift pockets along the bottom sides, two or four per side. 40 ft containers do not have forklift pockets but may instead feature a special gooseneck tunnel for securing onto truck trailers. Additionally, some containers have a recess along the bottom side rails which allows them to be lifted with special straddle carriers (commonly used at intermodal facilities).

Container floors consists of 28 mm thick 19 ply treated plywood screwed into structural cross members. They are capable of carrying a fork-lift truck with a maximum axle load of 12,040 lbs, if the contact area between wheels is at least 22 sq. inches. This factor is regulated by ISO 1496/I.

The maximum floor load should not exceed:

20' containers > 4 tons per 3 sq ft, 40' containers > 3 tons per 3 sq ft

Stack-ability

Containers are stackable eight-high (eight floors for a container structure -68ft high). While stacking this high is not something utilized by small container buildings, it does encourage conceptualizing apartment or condominium pod buildings made from containers. The stackable design of shipping containers allows them to stand on another same size container by way of contact with the corner fittings. The lower corner fittings are generally flush with the lower side rails. The upper corner fittings extrude above the upper side rails and roof panels slightly to prevent contact between the roof and cross members of another stacked container.

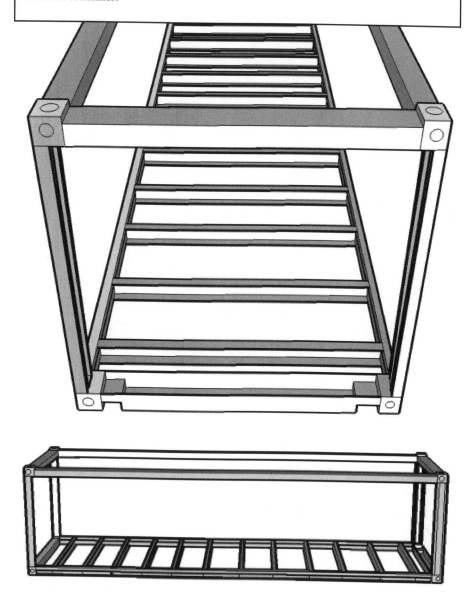

Dimensions & Capacities of Typical (late model) General Purpose Steel Dry Cargo Containers

	40 Foot Typical	40 Foot High Cube	20 Foot Typical	20 Foot High Cube
External Length	40' 12,192mm	40' 12,192mm	19'10 1/2" 6,058mm	19'10 1/2" 6,058mm
External Width	8' 2,438mm	8' 2,438mm	8' 2,438mm	8' 2,438mm
External Height	8'6" 2,591mm	9'6" 2,896mm	8'6" 2,591mm	9'6" 2,896mm
Internal Length	39' 4 13/64" 12,032mm	39' 4 13/64" 12,032mm	19'4 13/64" 5,898mm	19'4 13/64" 5,898mm
Internal Width	7' 8 33/64" 2,350mm	7' 8 33/64" 2,350mm	7' 8 33/64" 2,350mm	7' 8 33/64" 2,350mm
Internal Height	7'10 3/32" 2,390mm	8'10 3/32" 2,695mm	7'10 3/32" 2,390mm	8'10 3/32" 2,695mm
Doorway Width	7' 8 3/64" 2,338mm	7' 8 3/64" 2,338mm	7' 8 3/64" 2,338mm	7' 8 3/64" 2,338mm
Doorway Height	7' 5 49/64" 2,280mm	8' 5 49/64" 2,585mm	7' 5 49/64" 2,280mm	8' 5 49/64" 2,585mm
Internal Cubic Capacity	2390 cu. ft 67.7 cu.m	2698 cu. ft 76.4 cu.m	1,170 cu.ft 33.1 cu.m	1,320 cu.ft 37.4 cu.m
Empty Weight	8,070 lbs 3,660 kg	8,470 lbs 3,840 kg	4,755 lbs 2,155 kg	5,070 lbs 2,300 kg
Maximum Payload	59,130 lbs 26,820 kg	58,730 lbs 26,640 kg	62,445 lbs 28,325 kg	62,130 lbs 28,180 kg

Gooseneck tunnel dimensions (40' only) : Length 3,315mm > Width 1,029mm > Height/Depth 120mm

The length, width, and height of containers is measured on the outside edges of the corner fittings. These are the longest, widest, and highest points.

Additional shipping container information, sketchup models, and various PDF manuals are available for free download on my website www.paulsawyers.com

40 foot

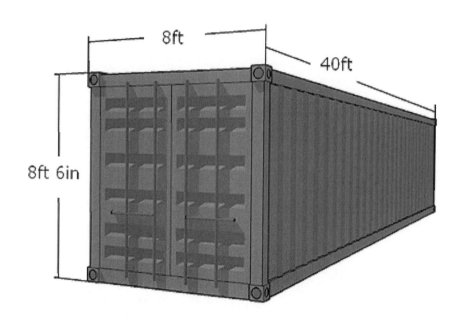

20 foot

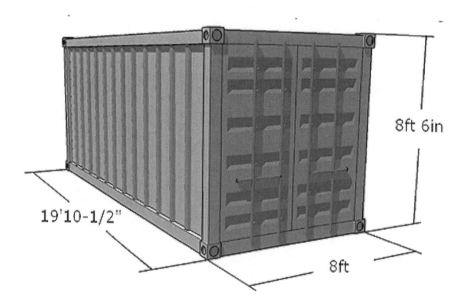

Standard Container

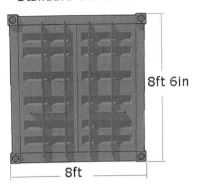

8ft 6in

8ft

High Cube Container

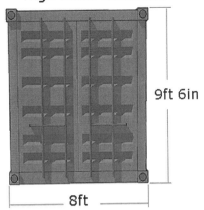

9ft 6in

8ft

Steel Container Exploded View

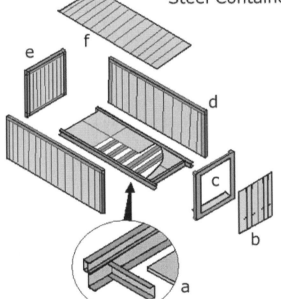

a) Container base, cross members, plywood flooring.

b) Door assembly.

c) Rear-end frame.

d) Top-side rail, side panel assembly.

e) Front-end frame.

f) Roof panel.

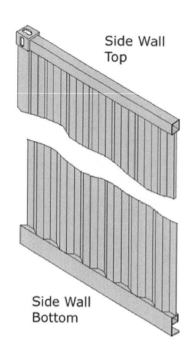

Side Wall
Top

Side Wall
Bottom

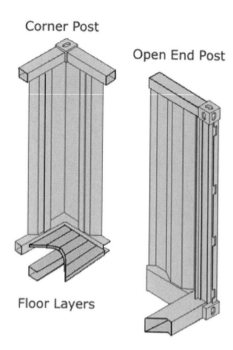

Corner Post

Open End Post

Floor Layers

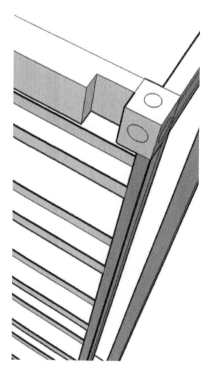

Corner Fitting

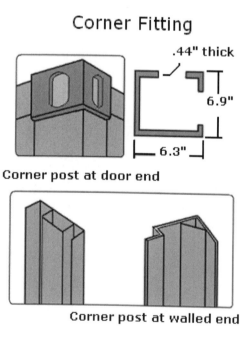

.44" thick

6.9"

6.3"

Corner post at door end

Corner post at walled end

Additional Specifications for Typical (late model) General Purpose Steel Dry Cargo Containers

20 ft Container Additional Specifications

Protrusions of Corner Fittings Beyond Container Body

Shipping containers are measured at the longest and widest points. These points are the corner fittings which extend slightly beyond the body of the container as follows.

a) The top of corner fittings protrude 6 mm above the highest point of the corrugated roof panel assembly.

b) The lower faces of the cross members are on a plane 12.5 mm +5/-1.5 mm above the lower faces of the bottom corner fittings.

c) The outside faces of corner fittings protrude from the outside faces of the corner post by 4 mm. The outside faces of the corner fittings protrude from the outside faces of the side walls by nominal 8 mm.

Component Dimensions

Bottom Side Rails
Qty : 2
Shape : Channel Section
Dimension : 48 x 158 x 30 x 4.5 mm

Forklift Pockets
Most 20 ft containers have forklift pockets built from 3 mm and 6 mm thick steel. These are built into the lower cross member assembly.

Cross Members
Shape : " C " section
Small one : 40 x 122 x 40 x 4.0 mm , Qty : 16
Large one : 75 x 122 x 45 x 4.5 mm , Qty : 2

Front End Wall
Thickness: 1.6 mm
Corrugation dimension- Outer face : 110 mm , Depth : 45.6 mm
Inner face : 104 mm , Slope : 18 mm

Front End Frame
Consists of one front sill, two corner posts, one front header and four corner castings.

Front Sill
Consists of "L" section steel and a square tube front rail on top.
"L" section plate : 4.0 mm thick.
Front rail : 60 x 60 x 3.0 mm

Corner Post
Corner posts are made using 6.0 mm thick section steel.

Front Header
Lower rail : 60 x 60 x 3.0 mm
Upper part : 3.0 mm thick

Rear End
Consists of one door sill, two corner posts, one rear header with header plate and four corner fittings, and the doors.

Corner Post
Inner part : 113 x 40 x 10 mm
Outer part : 6.0 mm thick

Door Header
Rear header : 4.0 mm thick
Header plate : 3.0 mm thick

Door Assembly
Two door leaves, two locking devices, four hinges and pins, seal gaskets and the door holders. The doors are capable of opening 270 degrees.

Door Leaves
1) Door panel :
thickness : 1.6 mm
2) Door frame :
a) Vertical door member: 100 x 50 x 3.2 mm
b) Horizontal door member: 150 x 50 x 3.0 mm

Roof Panels
Camber upwards : 6 mm
Panel thickness : 1.6 mm
Sheet Qty : 5 pieces

Roof Reinforcement Plates
Four 3.0 m thick reinforcement plates are be mounted around the four corner fittings.

Side Wall Components

Top Side Rails
Each top side rail is a 60 x 60 x 3.0 mm square steel pipe.

Side Walls
a) Inner panels : 1.6 mm thick ±
b) Outer panels : 2.0 mm thick ±

± Sidewall panels range from 1.6mm-2.0mm thick. Each side wall is comprised of a solid panel (1.6mm-2.00mm thick), or a series of panel sheets, depending on manufacture. When the side wall panel is built with a series of sheets, the "outer" sheets (which make contact with the corner posts) are a thicker steel (2mm). This is an engineering tactic that creates additional strength. The "inner" panels are slightly thinner (1.6mm) steel and comprise 80% of the span starting from the center and working outward toward the corner posts. These type of panel sheets are butt welded together using automatic welding to form one continuous panel. This further illustrates how the sidewall is a major structural aspect and care must be taken when removing portions of it. It's best to remove only portions from the center, if at all.

Floor

The Floor Boards
Plywood treated with preservative (required by the Commonwealth Department of Health, Australia).
Plywood thickness : 28 mm
Plywood ply number : 19
Plywood material : Apitong, Keruing, (or other Asian hardwood)
Glue : Phenol-formaldehyde resin
Preservative: BASILEUM SI-84 or others

The plywood boards are secured to each cross member with self-tapping zinc plated steel screws. The screws are countersunk 2 mm deep. Screws : 8.0 mm diameter shank x 16 mm diameter head x 45 mm length

40 ft Container Additional Specifications

Protrusions of Corner Fittings Beyond Container Body
Shipping containers are measured at the longest and widest points. These points are the corner fittings which extend slightly beyond the body of the container as follows.

a) The top of corner fittings protrude 6 mm above the highest point of the corrugated roof panel assembly.

b) The lower faces of the cross members are on a plane 17 mm above the lower faces of the bottom corner fittings.

c) The outside faces of corner fittings protrude from the outside faces of the corner post by 3 mm. The outside faces of the corner fittings protrude from the outside faces of the side walls by nominal 7 mm.

Component Dimensions

Bottom Side Rails
Qty : 2
Shape : Channel Section
Dimension : 162 x 48 x 30 x 4.5 mm

Cross Members
Shape : " C " section
Small one : 122 x 45 x 40 x 4.0 mm , Qty : 25
Large one : 122 x 75 x 40 x 4.0 mm , Qty : 3

Gooseneck Tunnel Parts (40 ft only)
a) Tunnel plate thickness : 4.0 mm Qty : 1
b) Tunnel bow thickness : 4.0 mm Qty : 12
c) Bolster thickness: 150 x 100 x 4.0 mm, Qty : 1
d) Outriggers - "C" section: 118 x 75 x 40 x 4.0 mm, Qty : 1/each side
118 x 45 x 40 x 4.0 mm, Qty : 7/each side

Front End Wall
Thickness: 1.6 mm
Corrugation dimension- Outer face : 110 mm , Depth : 45.6 mm
Inner face : 104 mm , Slope : 18 mm

Front End Frame
Consists of one front sill, two corner posts, one front header and four corner castings.

Front Sill
Consists of "L" section steel and a square tube front rail on top.
"L" section plate : 4.0 mm thick.
Front rail : 60 x 60 x 3.0 mm

Corner Post
Corner posts are made using 6.0 mm thick section steel.

Front Header
Lower rail : 60 x 60 x 3.0 mm
Upper part : 3.0 mm thick

Rear End
Consists of one door sill, two corner posts, one rear header with header plate
and four corner fittings, and the doors.

Door Sill
a) Door sill : 4.5 mm thick Slope : 1:10 approx.
b) Stiffener ribs : 4.5 mm thick Qty : 4 pieces

Corner Post
Inner part : 113 x 40 x 12 mm
Outer part : 6.0 mm thick

Door Header
Rear header : 4.0 mm thick
Header plate : 3.0 mm thick

Door Assembly
Two door leaves, two locking devices, four hinges and pins, seal gaskets and
the door holders. The doors are capable of opening 270 degrees.

Door Leaves
1) Door panel : Depth : 36 mm
Inner face : 72 mm
Slope : 68 mm
Panel thickness : 2.0 mm
2) Door frame : a) Vertical door member: 100 x 50 x 3.2 mm
b) Horizontal door member: 150 x 50 x 3.0 mm

Side Wall Components

Top Side Rails
Each top side rail is a 60 x 60 x 3.0 mm square steel pipe.

Side Walls

a) Inner panel : 1.6 mm thick (9 panels each side) ±
b) Outer panel : 2.0 mm thick (2 panels each side) ±
c) Corrugation shape:
Outer face : 72 mm , Slope : 68 mm
Inner face : 70 mm , Depth : 36 mm

± Sidewall panels range from 1.6mm-2.0mm thick. Each side wall is comprised of a solid panel (1.6mm-2.00mm thick), or a series of panel sheets, depending on manufacture. When the side wall panel is built with a series of sheets, the "outer" sheets (which make contact with the corner posts) are a thicker steel (2mm). This is an engineering tactic that creates additional strength. The "inner" panels are slightly thinner (1.6mm) steel and comprise 80% of the span starting from the center and working outward toward the corner posts. These type of panel sheets are butt welded together using automatic welding to form one continuous panel. This further illustrates how the sidewall is a major structural aspect and care must be taken when removing portions of it. It's best to remove only portions from the center, if at all.

Roof Panels

Corrugation Shape - Depth : 20 mm , Pitch : 209 mm
Inter face : 91 mm , Slope : 13.5 mm
Outer face : 91 mm
Camber upwards : 5 mm
Panel thickness : 2.0 mm
Sheet Qty : 11 pieces

Roof Reinforcement Plates

Four 3.0 m thick reinforcement plates are be mounted around the four corner fittings.

Floor

The Floor Boards

Plywood treated with preservative (required by the Commonwealth Department of Health, Australia).
Plywood thickness : 28 mm
Plywood ply number : 19
Plywood material : Apitong, Keruing, (or other Asian hardwood)
Glue : Phenol-formaldehyde resin
Preservative: BASILEUM SI-84 or others

The plywood boards are secured to each cross member with self-tapping zinc plated steel screws. The screws are countersunk 2 mm deep. Screws : 8.0 mm diameter shank x 16 mm diameter head x 45 mm length

2. Purchase and Delivery of Containers

Availability of containers for sale depends upon many factors including but not limited to where you live, current international trade agreements, current cost of oil, current cost of raw materials (steel), current supply of and demand for containers, also the current state of affairs in China (the largest current exporter and manufacturer of shipping containers). In the United States containers for sale are plentiful due to the fact that the U.S. imports out number it's exports by a high ratio. Many of the containers end up for sale at some point. This may not be the case where you live.

A simple comparison of container popularity worldwide shows you the types of containers you are most likely to find for sale. In 1995 Containerization International reported these global numbers of active containers:

89,800 - 20 ft steel dry cargo units 8 ft in height

7,200 - 20 ft steel dry cargo units 9-1/2 ft in height (high cube)

3,354,000 - 20 ft steel dry cargo units 8-1/2 ft in height.

These statistics are similar for 40 ft units. This illustrates how dominant the 8-1/2 ft high containers are. Using a 1995 statistic of (the then) newer containers provides a good idea of the now available used ones.

The general public can purchase new or used containers from brokers or resellers in most states. You do not need to live in a port city or a city located near a rail hub, containers can be delivered directly to your construction site via truck. You will be charged per mile for delivery and those further from the source will pay accordingly. Current cost of fuel will play a role in the delivery charge. Used shipping containers for sale on Ebay offer prospective buyers a ballpark idea of what to expect cost-wise. New containers can be found from dealers via Google. Many of the larger corporations in the container sales business operate nation-wide locations and can deliver units via dispatch to all states.

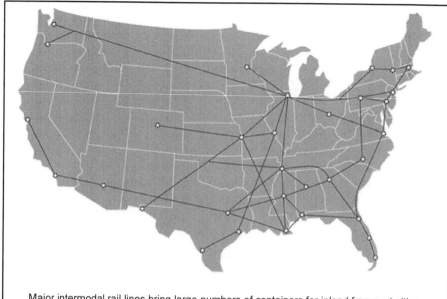

Major intermodal rail lines bring large numbers of containers far inland from port cities.

Containers for sale in regional classified newspaper

There are many ways to locate and purchase new or used shipping containers. Websites like Google and Ebay are good places to start.

You can also look through the phone book under 'shipping', 'containerized freight', 'mobile storage', 'shipping containers' or 'freight shipping' for local sales outlets.

Buyers should be provided a reasonable opportunity for pre-purchase inspection of actual units being purchased, units in similar used condition, or at the very least a visual (photo) representation of the expected used condition of units to be delivered.

Prospective buyers are advised to examine any sales contracts carefully and to retain a right of refusal if units arrive in a poorer than represented condition. Buyers can always inspect containers prior to purchase and delivery if the reseller has them on hand to view.

Top 20 U.S. Intermodal Ports 2003-2006, in TEUs

Ranking	Ports	2006	2005	2004	2003
1	Los Angeles	5,719,497	4,867,073	4,897,346	4,709,339
2	Long Beach	4,792,772	4,395,942	3,716,775	3,114,221
3	New York	3,672,643	3,390,308	3,146,569	2,819,407
4	Savannah	1,602,339	1,482,728	1,287,550	1,130,581
5	Charleston	1,510,869	1,511,935	1,401,522	1,252,674
6	Norfolk	1,419,327	1,318,831	1,200,244	1,095,579
7	Oakland	1,410,533	1,372,231	1,192,487	1,070,474
8	Houston	1,289,841	1,231,186	1,090,571	943,459
9	Seattle	1,223,266	1,339,641	1,044,270	818,684
10	Tacoma	1,095,316	1,154,350	937,202	936,951
11	Miami	746,869	770,839	801,290	771,362
12	P. Ever-glades	637,694	580,179	499,696	429,315
13	Baltimore	405,802	380,574	352,254	309,172
14	San Juan	213,162	213,570	199,751	188,380
15	New Orleans	176,645	174,072 *	242,272	236,439
16	Philadelphia	175,570	158,706	132,581	104,278
17	Wilmington	169,449	161,645	148,158	195,153
18	Portland	168,095	120,928	209,048	211,744
19	Gulfport	161,635	150,205 *	189,831	174,957
20	Jacksonville	153,009	144,635	144,074	118,552
Top 20	Total	26,744,283	24,959,465	22,780,840	20,559,528

* Represents a drop-off in container volume as a direct result of infrastructure damage caused by hurricane Katrina.

Ranking based on 2006 reported TEU counts.

Inspection Checklist

1) Cracks, breaks, cuts, tears, punctures, corrosion in corner fitting joints, side-wall joints, and floors cross member structure.
2) Missing, cracked, or broken welds at any major structural juncture.
3) Loose or missing fasteners at any major structural juncture.
4) Any deformations such as dents, bends, or bowing.
5) Check for old repairs such as welded on steel patches.

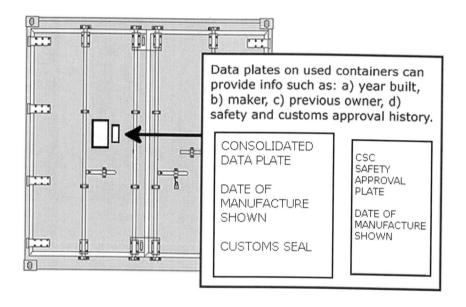

Data plates on used containers can provide info such as: a) year built, b) maker, c) previous owner, d) safety and customs approval history.

CONSOLIDATED DATA PLATE

DATE OF MANUFACTURE SHOWN

CUSTOMS SEAL

CSC SAFETY APPROVAL PLATE

DATE OF MANUFACTURE SHOWN

Delivery

The logical way to start your container building project is to come up with a plan for your building, deciding if you want to use 20 or 40 foot units. 40 ft containers are more common and do not cost much that more. Flat bed trucks can deliver one 40 ft unit, or two 20 ft units. So, you will pay more in delivery fees when using 40 ft units (that is, if you require more than one 40 ft unit be delivered).

The next step is to locate possible containers for purchase. Once you have a source for purchasing your units, plan out and install your foundation (see chapter 3 for more about building foundations). Then you can pay for the containers and arrange for delivery after concrete (if using a concrete foundation) cures. This is also a good time to check into renting a truck mounted (boom) crane to place units on the foundation.

Foundation Construction and Delivery Coordination

Concrete footings and slab foundations should be planned and installed prior to taking delivery of your containers.

Builders need to consider what type of trailer their containers will arrive on, roll-bed or standard. Also, will a crane rental be on-site at the same time (for transfer of containers onto the foundation)? Will you need to rent the crane two separate times? How long will it take for your concrete foundation to cure (when can it support the containers)?

Make sure to coordinate all the details of 1) foundation construction, 2) delivery date, and delivery vehicle, and 3) crane rental. All three aspects must work in concert for a smooth transition of your containers from delivery truck to permanent concrete foundation.

Containers are usually delivered via flat bed, if you have a crane to unload it at your location, or by tilt-bed if you prefer it dropped. Container tilt-bed trailers allow the container to slide off at the desired location. The driver backs the trailer and lower the end of the container until it touches the ground then pulls straight out from under the container.

Deliveries require a fairly level, smooth, and firm surface (the truck and trailer weigh over 30,000 lb.). Most companies can deliver on dirt, cement, pavement, asphalt, gravel or grass as long as it is not too soft.

For a 20 ft storage container, you will need approximately 50 feet of straight clearance. For a 40 ft container, you will need approximately 100 feet of straight clearance. The width requirement is approximately 12 feet.

You should have at least 14 feet of overhead clearance on the road to the delivery site and 20 feet at the drop off location. Any obstacles like trees and overhead wires must be cleared prior to delivery.

It is possible drag a 20 ft container short distances using a 3/4 ton pickup truck. Attempting to drag a 40 ft container is not advised.

Delivery drivers are often flexible, and may go off-road to drop your unit in the spot you desire. Of course there are limits to this. The truck and container weighs enough to sink into and become stuck in ground that is not firm and dry. This may restrict your delivery options seasonally.

Some companies use specialized delivery trucks for 20' containers. These are called side-loaders and drop the container on the passenger side of the truck with hydraulic arms. These vehicles are usually able to reach a more back-woods location than a semi towing a flat bed trailer.

If no arrangements for a special delivery truck have been made, you will need to hire a crane capable of lifting the container off the flat bed trailer and onto your foundation, and have it waiting on site at delivery. The expense of hiring heavy equipment will be worthwhile, and still bring your structure together for a low cost.

The 20 ft container with forklift pockets can be lifted and placed with a rough terrain forklift. Some container deliveries come with this heavy duty forklift and operator. They are usually high reach models capable of stacking first floor containers on footings and placing second level units on top of those.

Most local equipment rental yards have a truck mounted crane available. These are usually the Terex telescopic boom crane type trucks, and can be operated by a regular civilian much like renting a moving van.

The compact truck mounted crane or 'boom truck' is the preferred method of unloading and stacking containers in small scale building situations.

A medium sized excavator is usually capable of lifting 20,000 lbs 30 ft high, and can also be used for container movement if a crane is not available.

Chains, hooks, cables, and lifting straps are connected to the excavators shovel for lifting. The excavator can be used for 2 level container stacking, or for creation of underground container based bomb shelters, but a crane is required for most other container building projects.

Corner fittings will accept common lifting hardware. Cranes often come stocked with an assortment of hooks, and basic lifting equipment.

If you need to purchase lifting hardware, Northern Tool (www.northerntool.com) is a good source for hooks, straps, and general devices.

Typical Telescopic Boom Truck Mounted Crane Specifications

Terex Stinger Model	Maximum Lift Capacity	Maximum Boom Length
2000	20,000 lbs	57 ft
2400	24,000 lbs	63 ft
3000	30,000 lbs	63 ft

Tip: Lay pieces of scrap 2x8 lumber down on top of concrete footings to absorb any sudden impact they may encounter during placement of the container via heavy equipment. Use a tractor jack to raise container and remove these later.

Placement order using crane

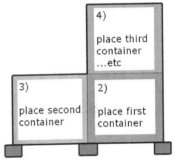

1) build foundation

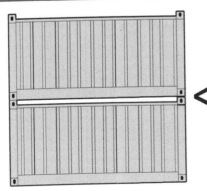

Upper corner fittings protrude 6 mm above the highest point of the roof panels.

Lower corner fittings are generally flush with the bottom side rails.

These aspects create a stackable design that protects the roofs of each container.

Industry Insider Interview Regarding Purchase and Delivery of Containers

Below are a few questions I asked Jim from Sea Box, Inc. (www.seabox.com). Special thanks to Jim for taking the time to participate.

Paul: How does the current price of steel and the scrap steel market affect container prices?

Jim: The current price of steel has dramatically affected the price of all new steel containers. Another factor that has caused a price fluctuation is the huge jump in new builds. This has caused a major increase in the price of used containers. The scrap steel market has no effect on the price fluctuation of used containers.

Paul: What are the future expectations regarding shipping container use and overall availability in North America?

Jim: The future of used container availability in North America should show a slight increase in supply. Several major steamship lines have large quantities of aging equipment which must be replaced soon.

Paul: What are your future expectations for shipping container structures?

Jim: More customers each month find ISO containers can be modified to transform into shelters, control rooms, work shops, structure container houses, art sculptures, large buildings, and special equipment enclosures, to house generator sets, water purification, sensing equipment and training centers.

Paul: Do you sell container related hardware such as clamps and lifting hooks for corner fittings?

Jim: We do sell container related hardware, such as deck mount twist locks and fastening devices, that are sold for boxes used as structures, not stacking on container ships. The more common accessories that we sell are HVAC, insulation, man doors, storage shelves and cabinets.

Paul: What types (if any) of specialized container delivery trailers do you utilize?

Jim: The types of delivery trailers that we utilize are 48' hydraulic tilt trailers and roll back and till back trucks, hook loaders, side loads and bogie towing.

Paul: Do you see any new trends emerging in delivery equipment?

Jim: I do not see any new trends (other than side loaders) emerging in the trailer/ delivery equipment area.

Paul: What are your terrain requirements for rural delivery?

Jim: We ask that areas be dry and cleared.

Paul: Can buyers who live away from intermodal ports and hubs still get a good deal on containers?

Jim: People in land-locked states can still get a good deal on containers. Their prices average only 10% higher in large inland cities compared to port cities. They would only pay a big delivery fee if demand exceeded local supply.

3. Footings and Foundations

Permanent footings and foundations should be planned and installed prior to taking delivery of your containers. Builders need to consider what type of trailer their containers will arrive on, roll-bed or standard. Also, will a crane be on-site at the same time for transfer of containers onto the foundation? Will you need to rent the crane two separate times? How long will it take for your concrete foundation to cure (when can it support the containers)? Make sure to coordinate all the details of 1) foundation construction, 2) delivery date, and delivery vehicle, and 3) crane rental. All three aspects must work in concert for a smooth transition of your containers from delivery truck to permanent concrete foundation.

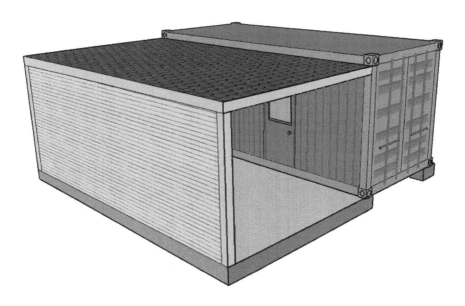

The overall integrity of your container structure will be improved by using a pre-planned foundation. This is not an absolute requirement, but using some type of foundation is advised. Raising your container's off the ground will reduce the corrosive effects of moisture over time.

Wood footings are a basic improvement over no footings at all. They are cheap and easy to install. Pressure treated lumber, or 'skids', can be placed under a container after mild site preparation.

Material for use as wood beam footings: 1) double stacked pressure treated 2x6's, 2) double stacked pressure treated 2x8's, 3) pressure treated 4x4's, 4) pressure treated or oiled railroad ties and other beams 6" x 6" or larger.

Most 20 ft shipping container buildings utilize concrete footings placed at a ratio of one per corner fitting. 40 ft buildings have one footing per corner but can also benefit from a mid-span footing .

The load bearing aspects of each containers corner posts are transferred directly to the footing and into the ground. Besides the corner posts, the bottom sides of containers run at a point close to flush and are able to rest on a single level plane. Mid-span footings built level with corner footings will provide a level plane for the bottom rails and corner fittings.

Concrete footings are low cost and they can be built by a single individual in their spare time, perhaps one per weekend, in preparation for a future container delivery date.

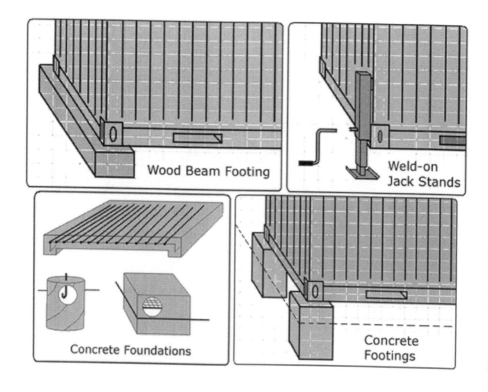

Wood Beam Footing

Weld-on Jack Stands

Concrete Foundations

Concrete Footings

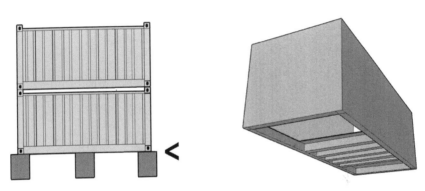

Container bottom rails are close to level with the ground and the bottom of the corner fittings. This trait depends on the model and year of container. In general, lower side rails range from perfectly flush to several mm higher than flush with the corner fittings.

This is important if you plan to install mid-span footings on the lower side rail (perhaps because you are removing a side wall etc). My feeling on this is go ahead and build all of your footings to the same height and use shims later if required. Plate steel in a variety of thickness can be utilized for shims if welding anchor plates is required. Plywood works well as a shim if you are not welding your containers down to the footings with anchor plates.

Concrete Footings

When it comes to footings, the higher the container rests, the easier many later tasks will be. Concrete footings 2-3 ft above the ground create the preferred foundation for a container structure. Footings of this height will help keep the bottom dry and free from corrosion. Creating a crawl space under your building will allow easy access to install mid-span support piers, conduit and future inspection and maintenance. For a relatively low investment a crawl space also provides double your covered storage square footage for the many items that will fit under a 2-3 ft height.

Containers generally only require support at each of the four corners, however, when large portions of side wall material is removed, the lower side rails could experience high levels of vertical stress (especially in 40 ft containers) at the mid-span point. Possible bowing could occur. This phenomenon is compounded when a second level of containers are placed on first level units with inner side walls removed. All buildings with side walls removed should receive footings under the mid-span point. When side wall material is removed, it is advised that builders install a steel or timber mid-span support beam (see chapter 4). This support can transfer stress directly through the mid span footing and into the ground

Containers make contact and stand primarily on the corner fittings, but lower corner fittings are generally flush with the lower side rails (and the ground) allowing them to stack flatly across level footings [see photo above of flush lower side rails]. Steel plate shims can be used if a footing does not reach it's planned position .

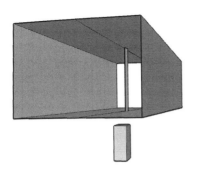

'Mid-span' supports transfer weight down beams, into footings, and finally into the ground.

If side wall material is removed from an existing structure and additional mid-span support is required, you can install pre-made adjustable concrete piers with 4x4 post brackets. These can be placed under an existing container building at the mid-span point and tightened to the required height. An array of four adjustable piers and 4x4 posts can be assembled to create a heavy duty mid-span support that will transfer extreme stress to the ground. If your structure is very low to the ground access for installing piers may be difficult. One solution is to remove a portion of the plywood to access the ground.

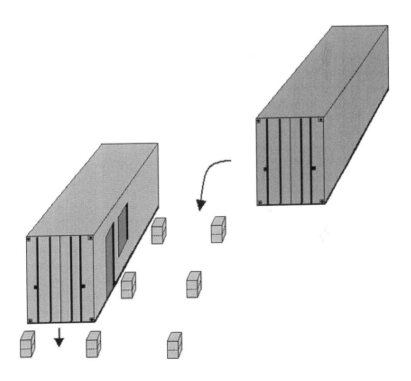

Number of Footings Required Per Container

If you are not removing large portions of side wall material, one footing per corner and corner fitting is adequate for most container buildings. Side walls are an integral part of the container and provide a good deal of strength via the corrugated ridges, so, when you remove them you have to make up for it with additional support; mid span support beams and footings.

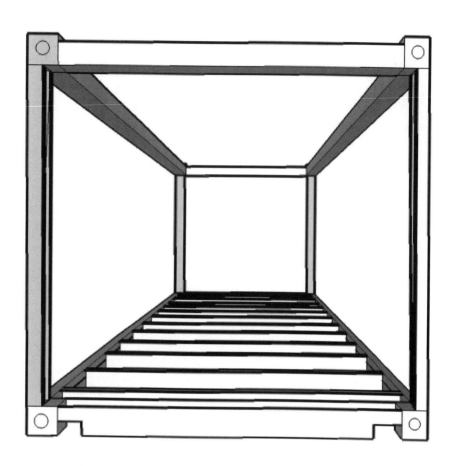

These images represent a basic idea of what's under a shipping container.

In addition to what you see in these drawings, 40 ft containers feature a 'goose neck tunnel' at one end for attachment to over the road trailers. 20 ft containers feature forklift pockets on the bottom side rails. These additional features usually play no role in aspects of container architecture.

The cross members are generally 3 mm thick C shaped steel. Each part is factory MIG welded together forming a very strong frame.

Footing Sizes

The first step in footing construction is figuring out how deep they should be. Footings can be prone to frost heave and this phenomenon will be the primary factor in deciding how deep to make them. Frost heave occurs only in very cold areas where the ground freezes. This results in a slight movement of the soil that can push up on the footing and structure resting upon it. Ask at your local building department if you are unsure of the frost line depth. If you live in an area where the ground does not freeze, you can skip over this step.

Footing forms should be dug out and poured to a depth of at least 6 in below ground in all climates. You will need a post hole digger for 2-3 ft deep holes and a power auger for 3-5 ft deep holes.

The remaining footing dimensions include overall height, width, and round or square. Like pizza, round or square is an important decision.

Round footings (also called columns or piers) are attractive and easy to build using readily available cardboard forming tubes. The forming tubes available at home improvement stores are usually designed for below-grade use, but may be poured to three feet above the ground line. No bracing is needed unless used two feet above ground line, even then, bracing requirements are minimal. Cardboard form tubes offer less view obstruction, no sharp corners to chip and break, and ease of installation.

Additional benefits of using tubular cardboard column forms:

Minimum bracing required.
Lightweight – easy to handle.
Good quality finish.
Can be cut on the job with a hand saw or circular saw.
With a form for each column, job progress can move as fast as desired.

In general, cardboard and lumber built footing forms offer a significant savings on costly concrete trucking charges due to the ability to schedule multiple pours in one day, as opposed to fiberglass or steel forms which require multiple days to pour, depending on the number of footings.

Container buildings that span 20 feet will rest safely on 12-inch-diameter piers, or 12 in. x 12 in. square footings. Container buildings that span 40 feet should receive larger 18-inch-diameter piers, or 18 in. x 18 in. square footings. These basic footing size guidelines should be considered the minimum. The more concrete you can put under a corner fitting the better.

Laying Out Foundations

The easiest and most precise method of mapping out exactly where to install footings is a laser level and square combo. This item can be purchased or rented for container building foundation layout.

Automatic self-leveling, 5 beam square and plum lasers generate perfect 90 degree laser beams that allow you to precisely stake corners and heights of footings for a square and level arrangement of footings that mate correctly with the container corner fittings. Corner fitting are approximately 6.5 in sq and will fit well on round or square footings built over 12 in. This provides room for adjustment.

The other way that is commonly used is the 3-4-5 method or 6-8-10 method. You measure up one 'leg' of the corner 3 ft and make a mark then measure up the other 'leg' 4 ft and make a mark. You then adjust the two 'legs' until the diagonal measures exactly 5 ft. When you do this it is then perfectly square.

On large buildings you would use 6 ft, 8 ft and 10 ft rather than the 3 ft, 4 ft and 5 ft as described.

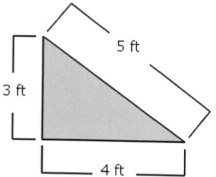

Formula for Finding the Center in Footing Placement

Container corner fittings are approximately 6.5 in square. There is one fitting on each side, thus the center of a corner fitting is the container width minus 6.5 in (or the container length minus 6.5 in).

Example

width >

96 in (8 ft) minus 3.25 in (half a corner fitting width),

minus 3.25 (half the other corner fitting width) = 89.5 in on center

Width minus 6.5 in = center of footing

Length minus 6.5 in = center of footing

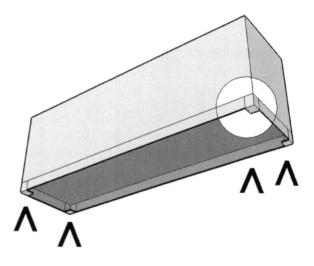

Pouring Footings Yourself vs. Hiring a Pre-Mix Truck

You can purchase 60-80 lb bags of pre mixed dry concrete to make footings yourself, but delivering the amount of bags required to your site will require a vehicle of significant capacity. Weekend builders can utilize smaller amounts of concrete by pouring single footings at their leisure. One single 80 lb bag of concrete yields a mere 2/3 of a cubic foot of finished concrete. This example shows how hiring a pre-mix truck to pour your footings certainly makes the job easier.

Concrete Estimating Formulas

Square footings... length x width x depth, divided by 1728 = cubic feet of concrete required to fill form

Round pier footings... radius (half the diameter) x itself (radius squared) x height x 3.14 divided by 1728 = cubic feet of concrete required to fill form

To convert cubic feet into the concrete ordering standard of cubic yards divide by 27. Some builders include an excess factor of 8% (divide by 25) to avoid a shortfall of material.

Round Tubes - Concrete Requirements

(expressed in cubic yards for columns of various heights)

Diameter (in.)	Height of Column		
	3 ft.	6 ft.	8 ft.
10	.061	.121	.162
12	.087	.176	.233
14	.119	.238	.317
16	.155	.310	.414
18	.196	.392	.523

Each 80 lb bag of ready mixed concrete yields: .66 cubic feet, or .022 cubic yards, of finished product.

Most concrete is sold in a 60-80 lb bag size, costing $3-$6 each. Most of these products produce high strength concrete, reaching 3000-4000 psi of compressive strength when cured.

Mixing can be accomplished in a shallow wheelbarrow but a portable mixer preferred. Mixers can be rented from your local rental facility or purchased (harbor freight .com sells low cost concrete mixers), but again, scheduling a concrete delivery is far easier.

Concrete Footing Forms

Shallow footings are ok for warmer climates

Deep forms must be dug out for cold areas

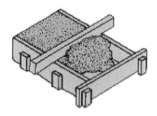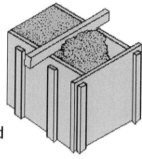

Form cavities are dug out and lined with sand or gravel

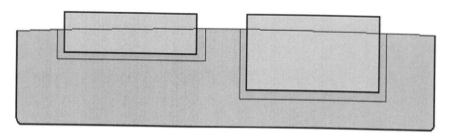

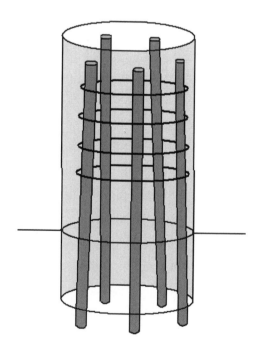

Concrete footing forms can be built and poured one per weekend by the casual builder in preparation for a future container building.

Once you have forms set in place you can insert rebar (slightly longer than the form) and hammer it into the ground beneath. Welded wire can also be shaped to fit within the form.

Anchoring Containers

The most popular method for anchoring containers to concrete footings is welding the lower corner fittings to an embedded steel plate. These welding (or anchoring) plates are usually made from 1/4 in to 5/8 in thick steel. The corner fittings are directly welded to these plates using 2-3 in angle.

Curved rebar or angle w/bolts is welded to the underside of the plates for submersion and embedding into the cement. Place a level on the plate immediately after embedding to check for level and correct as needed. Shims between the plate and footing form bay be required.

Steel weld-to plate for footing

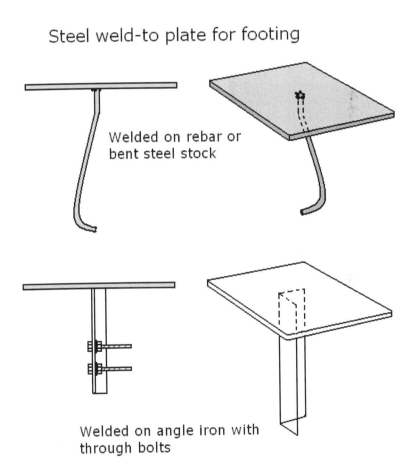

Welded on rebar or
bent steel stock

Welded on angle iron with
through bolts

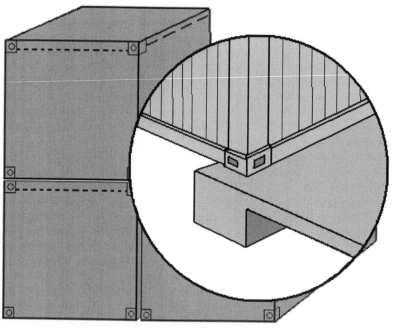

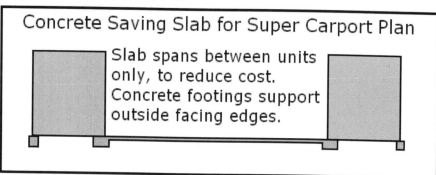

Concrete Saving Slab for Super Carport Plan

Slab spans between units only, to reduce cost. Concrete footings support outside facing edges.

Certain types of building designs such as carport and vehicle storage or service structures call for the installation of a concrete slab either between two containers or next to a single unit.

You can build these designs on a basic array of concrete footings and have the slab between poured at a later time. To save costs, you can substitute asphalt or gravel in place of a slab.

The forms and rebar for a slab can be installed by you, but in general, big concrete slabs are best poured by ready-mix truck and the accompanying crew.

Additional Footing Options

Adjustable concrete piers with 4x4 post brackets are a simple low cost solution
to many foundation problems. They can be installed quickly in a variety of man-
ners using various pieces of lumber. The adjustable aspect of these piers elimi-
nates many of the requirements for buildings placed on pre-built footings. Adjustable concrete piers with 4x4 post brackets are commonly available at home
improvement stores.

Automotive jack stands can be used on containers placed in existing asphalt or
concrete surfaces such as parking lots.

Weld-on adjustable jacks are also available. These offer the advantage of being
adjustable via a built-in worm gear and attachable hand crank. Lifting capacity
ranges from 7000 lbs to 10,000 per jack, and lifting range is from 22" to 54" depending on model. These are designed for welding onto your trailer, or in this
case, your container. They will probably require some fitting.

Army and Marine ISO Shelters feature these type of built-in jacks for adaptation
to a variety of terrain conditions.

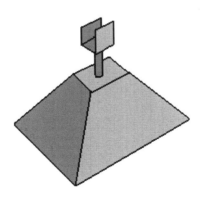

Adjustable Concrete Pier

4. Joining Containers

It's easy to turn a standard 8 ft wide container into a building, but this leaves you with only 7 ft 8 in. wide worth of interior space. Since containers can be stacked on top of one another or set next to each other, it's a natural move to incorporate that feature into your building.

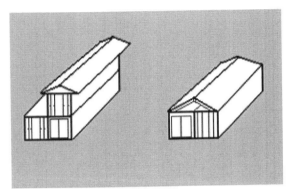

Most container structure plans call for some form of stacking or butting up of units. I am from the school of thought that containers should be stacked in the manner in which they are designed that is corner post to corner post on the corner fittings.

I am often asked about placing the end of a second level forty foot container onto the mid-section of a ground level container and so forth. The simple fact is these boxes were not designed to be stacked this way and layouts like this should avoided save for advanced engineers with plans to erect addition steel framework.

Corner-to-corner stacking and butting of containers is a process that follows construction of the footings. As mentioned in chapter two, a crane or boom truck crane is best used to place your containers on the footings and stack additional floors on top.

Containers placed side by side will make contact at the corner fittings leaving a small gap between the side walls. The process of sealing this gap (with roofing cement gasket) will take place at top and side rails as described in chapter 5.

Container design transmits the majority of stress during stacking to the vertical corner posts, but removal of the side wall material creates a significant loss of rigidity. In it's role moving tons of cargo, this would be disastrous for the container, but when used as a structure side wall removal works fine as proven by the many builds that feature it.

If you are planning to add a second floor unit, and have removed side wall material on the first floor units, you must install some support beams (on the first floor). You should also install footings under any mid-span supports to transfer the weigh to the ground.

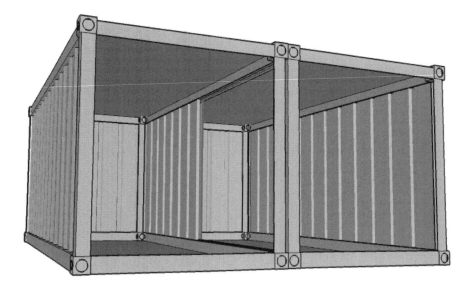

It is common in the container building world to remove all or part of the side wall material when joining containers together.

The obvious original benefit of this modification was a wider structure, but it also created enormous versatility, perhaps even the acceptance of shipping containers as serious architectural components due to the flexibility created.

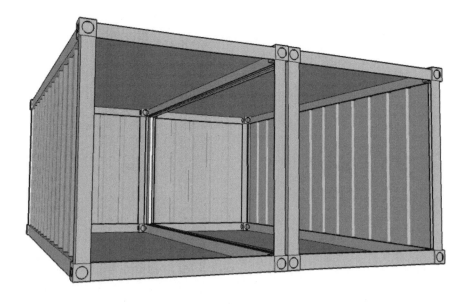

Corner fittings protrude 3-4mm from side walls

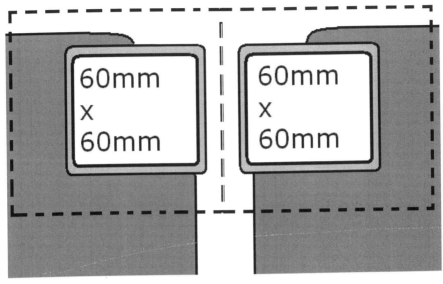

Corner fittings make contact before any other parts of a container touches. Hence, other parts of a container never touch. There is a gap between the corner posts and side wall material created by the protruding corner fittings.

On paper, the gap between containers butted together is only 6 mm - 8 mm. In reality this gap can vary from 10– 30 mm.

The goal is to butt containers as close as possible, weld various pieces of 1/4 in plate bridges across the corner posts, upper and lower side rails, then fill the remaining gap with roofing cement creating a giant gasket.

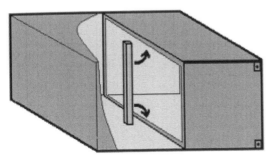

When constructing a two-wide building, the builder can choose to: **a)** remove (the joined) side walls yielding an interior with 16' of open space, **b)** remove a portion of (the joined) side walls, or **c)** keep (the joined) side walls intact.

Keeping the joined side walls intact will simplify the building process, but many who choose to build a side by side container structure, do so with the intent of removing the side walls thus creating a space larger than 8 ft wide. If the 8 foot width of unaltered containers is too small for your designs application, removal of side wall material is required. Once the side wall material is removed, you will need to seal the remaining seam where the two units meet.

You can cut the 14 gauge (.075") corrugated steel side panel material using a reciprocating saw or angle grinder.

Carefully remove segments of wall, then gradually trim out the inside edges in accordance with one of the two sealing techniques shown in this chapter. Large segments of side wall material can be saved for use as porch or door coverings.

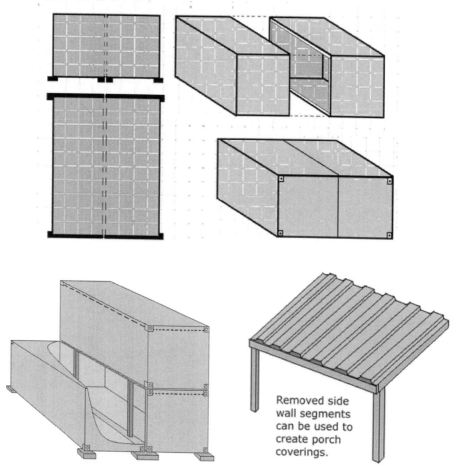

Removed side wall segments can be used to create porch coverings.

Joining Methods

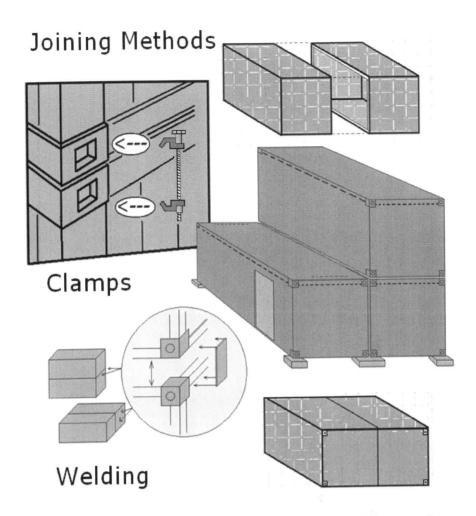

Clamps

Welding

The most popular method of anchoring containers together is welding... usually 1/4 in plate along the side rails, corner posts, and/or corner fittings. Welded plate can be applied to the exterior, but the preferred method is to install enough plate material to cover the entire joined seam from the inside. This later serves as a support shelf for application of roofing cement from the outside gap.

Common Types Steel Stock for Anchoring Containers Together

1018 Mild Steel
Available in plate, square bar, and rectangle bar.

A36 Mild Steel
Available in plate, square bar, rectangle bar, as well as steel shapes such as I-Beams, H-beams, angles, and channels. Note that its yield strength is also significantly less than 1018 - this means that it will bend much more quickly than will 1018. A36 steel cost less than 1018 steel.

A variety of materials can be used to join container together as shown on the next few pages. The strongest method is outlined below on this page.

Steel Plate Welded Over Entire Joined Seam Applied to Interior

With this method the builder works from the inside of the container out.

1/4 in steel plate is cut to size and welded over the entire joint seam from the inside. This later serves as a support shelf for application of roofing cement from the outside gap creating a giant gasket on the top and side gaps preventing water leaks.

This is not the easiest method of joining containers due to the extensive cutting of steel required. Easier methods are illustrated on the next few pages.

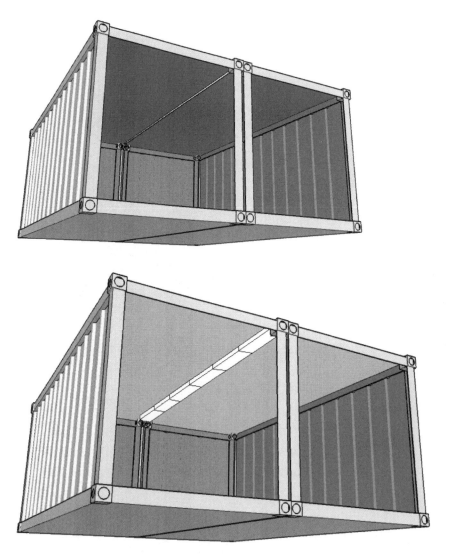

Joining Units Together Via Welds

Trim out steel walls leaving tops, sides, and floor flush with the tubular frame

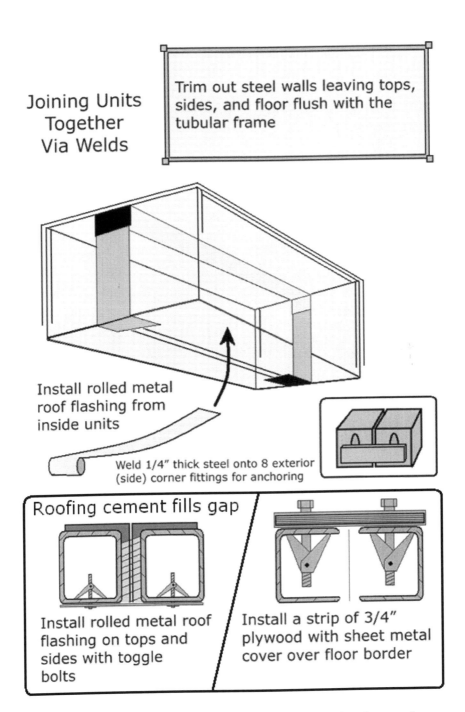

Install rolled metal roof flashing from inside units

Weld 1/4" thick steel onto 8 exterior (side) corner fittings for anchoring

Roofing cement fills gap

Install rolled metal roof flashing on tops and sides with toggle bolts

Install a strip of 3/4" plywood with sheet metal cover over floor border

Low cost options for welding container together usually involve small segments of welded plate at strategic locations like corner fittings followed by the application of sheet steel roofing and roofing cement materials to create a waterproof roof at the joined section.

Joining Units Together Via Bolts

Trim out steel walls leaving a 3-4" border on tops and sides

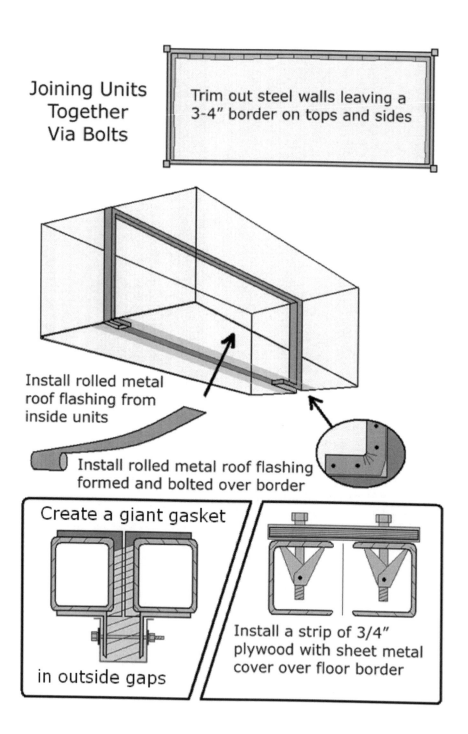

Install rolled metal roof flashing from inside units

Install rolled metal roof flashing formed and bolted over border

Create a giant gasket

in outside gaps

Install a strip of 3/4" plywood with sheet metal cover over floor border

It's possible to leave a small border when removing side walls and use it as a platform to bolt containers together in situations where welding is not desired.

You can create a passageway or doorway in side-walls without the addition of support beams.

Such a minor re-moval of side wall material has little effect on rigidity.

No weather proof-ing is needed if you plan to seal the roof as shown below.

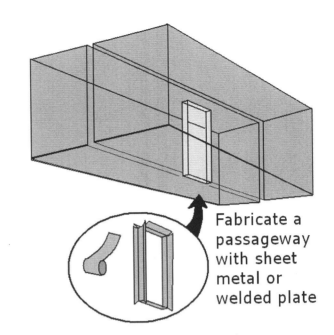

Fabricate a passageway with sheet metal or welded plate

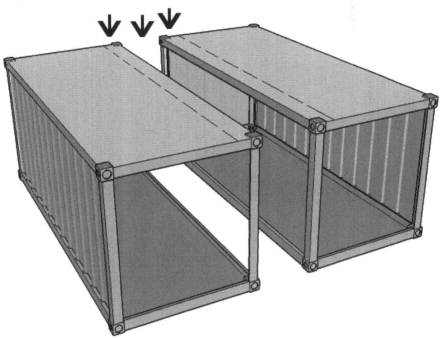

Roofing cement is commonly available in 5 gallon buckets at home improvement stores. It should be used liberally in conjunction with standard sheet roofing metals to form a tough water resistant gasket on the roof and sides of joined containers. This product is messy and tends to stick to everything it touches. You can use large size masking tape to create a clean line on the roof. The broken line in the above drawing is an example of how far out to apply roofing cement (the masking point).

Mid Span Supports with Footings

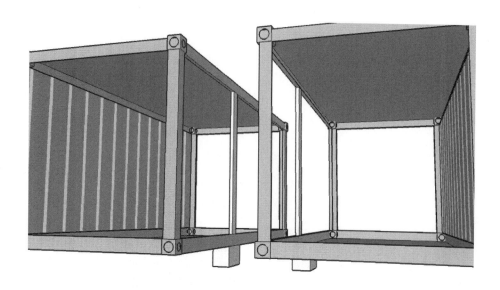

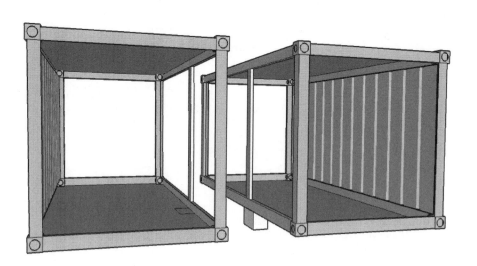

5. Roofing Containers

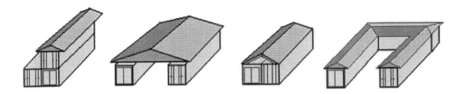

One of the attractions of container buildings is the fact that they do not require a roof. The downside of this is, void of constant movement, container roofs could gather leafs and snow between the corrugated segments.

Shipping containers are manufactured with a slightly curved corrugate steel roof that discourages water from pooling on it. Water will drain off a level container on the long sides.

Drainage is not a problem on a single wide container building setup but does present issues for side-by-side configurations.

One way to bypass this problem altogether is to construct an additional roof that spans the tops of two (or more) wide structures. Traditional building techniques and materials are used for these add-on roofs.

Installing a simple lumber built gable roof will eliminate any drainage, snow, and falling debris problems in one step.

Some container plans call for the addition of these simple gable roofs, but most do not. I feel an added roof improves the visual appeal, but this is a judgment call by the individual builder.

Roof options include keeping the ends of the roof open (the space under the roof can be used for storage), or enclosing the gable ends to create a interior accessible insulated storage space via a cut hatch-way in the roof panel.

Container roof panels will not support a great deal of weight, but are useful for storing lightweight bulky items such as hoses, tubing, kayaks, camping gear and so forth.

Storage for bulky
lightweight items
can be gained by
creating a loft

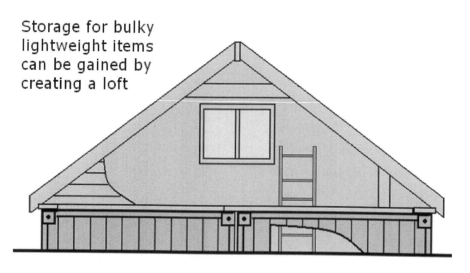

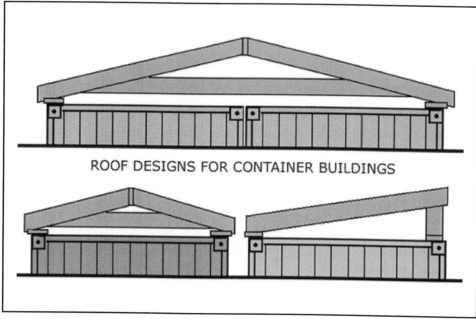

ROOF DESIGNS FOR CONTAINER BUILDINGS

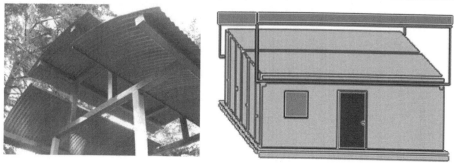

Container Roofs vs. Extreme Heat & Cold

One of the major benefits of adding a roof to a container structure is additional insulation. The roof can reduce heat or cold felt inside the building considerably. This will likely be an absolute requirement in extreme climates.

Traditional gable roofs can be built fully closed-in with a standard interior access hatch just like a home. Proper vents and fiberglass insulation in this 'attic' space will act to control the climate inside a container structure. This type of roof and insulation, combined with LP or wood heat, and some form of side wall insulation will work well in cold climates.

Extra high and open roofs are a common method used to dissipate interior heat in very hot and humid tropical environments. Jungle container buildings often feature open-top containers or fully removed steel roof panels. Extra high lumber built roof structures containing large ventilated panels and windows are added to these open tops to create a well ventilated (and cooler) interior.

Why Roof Container Buildings ?

Direct sunlight on steel containers creates a large amount of heat rapidly.

Steel walls (and roofs) offer no heat retention qualities without insulation.

Roofs can span two spaced containers creating additional covered sq footage.

Roofs and siding can create the appearance of a traditional building.

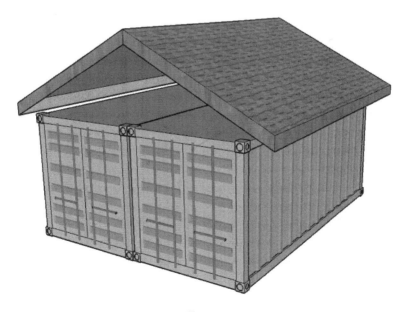

Options for building a roof over a single container or two container placed side-by-side are a gable roof or a flat sloped roof.

If building a carport style structure you will need to create a roof that spans two containers. The roof can be built to span just about any length within reason, with 12 ft being the easiest and commonly thought of as the minimal useful span between two containers.

There are four basic methods for building a roof span between two containers:

1) Full gable roof that attaches on the outside edges of the containers and spans the entire width of both containers.

2) Partial gable roof that attaches on the inside edges of the containers and spans a portion of each container.

3) Full flat roof that attaches on the outside edges of the containers and spans the entire width of both containers.

4) Partial flat roof that attaches on the inside edges of the containers and spans a portion of each container.

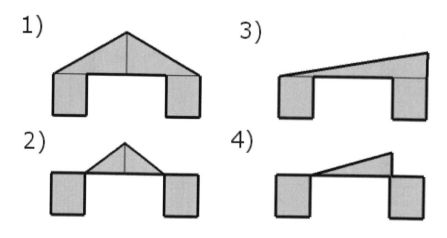

1) 3)

2) 4)

Establishing an Attachment Point for Top Plates

The first question that comes to mind after examining a containers top is where do you connect the base for attachment of the roof?

Some containers have the upper side rail covered on the outside with side wall material leaving only a small lip on the side.

More common is an exposed upper side rail with the side wall material welded directly to it.

The two hurdles to overcome are the protruding side rail (on the side) and the lack of level mounting space (on the top).

The roof panels will not provide a strong foundation for anchoring roof components, so the weight needs be placed on the side rails which are extremely strong 60 mm x 60 mm x 3 mm square steel pipes.

The top edge of a container does not offer a flush surface and only a few inches of space to mount structural top-plate material for roof construction.

One solution is to utilize (the nearest level surface) the corrugated side wall material as an attachment point for structural lumber.

Using this method you can bolt structural lumber (2x6s or 2x8s) directly to the very upper most part of the side walls. The lumber should butt up against the top side rail. This acts as a level starting point to build a long narrow base for attachment of roofing aspects.

Roofing Building Process

1) Mount top plate structural lumber
2) Install trusses or rafters
3) Install roofing

The top edge of a container does not offer a flush surface and only a few inches of space to mount structural top-plate material for roof construction.

One solution is to utilize (the nearest level surface) the corrugated side wall material as an attachment point for structural lumber. Using this method you can bolt structural lumber (2x6s or 2x8s) directly to the very upper most part of the side walls. The lumber should butt up against the top side rail.

This acts as a level starting point to build a long narrow base for attachment of roofing aspects.

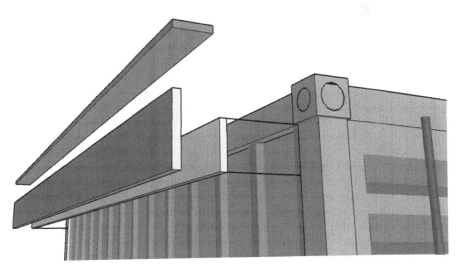

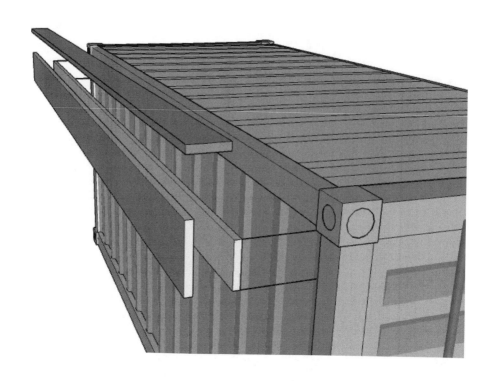

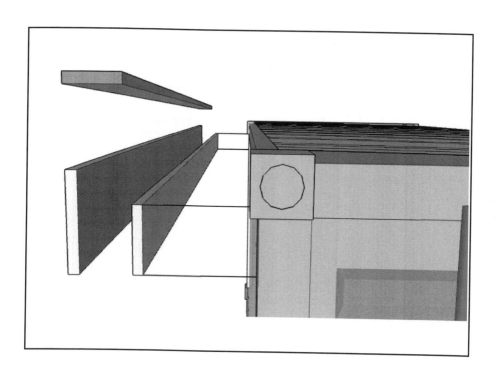

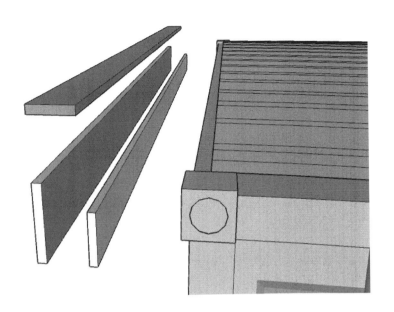

Rafter Installation

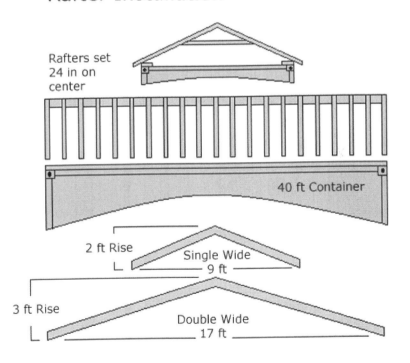

Rafters set 24 in on center

40 ft Container

2 ft Rise

Single Wide
9 ft

3 ft Rise

Double Wide
17 ft

Eaves & Roofing

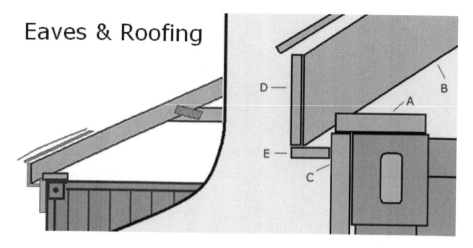

Roof Components

A) **Top plate**
B) **Rafter**
C) **Ledger**
D) **Fascia**
E) **Soffit**

Roofs can be finished with fascia and soffit boards to create a clean traditional look. Vents should be installed if you close-in the entire under roof area.

Actual roofing materials can be OSB, plywood, or a corrugated product as shown in the below photo. OSB and plywood with require shingles, steel roofing, or similar type product for completion of the roof.

Rafter built roof: rafters are notched and fastened to the 2x6 top plates.

Truss built roof: trusses are built at ground level then raised into position.

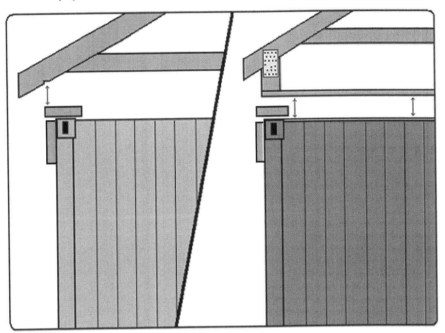

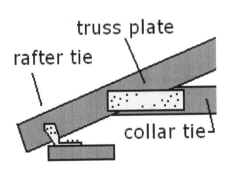

truss plate

rafter tie

collar tie

Roofs require lots of planning and are an obvious extra expense. You can establish a side-by-side shipping container building on footings, seal the seam, and build the roof at a later time when funds are available. The best way to avoid water leaks between joined containers is to create a giant gasket made of roofing cement.

Roofing cement is a low cost asphalt based material readily available in five gallon buckets at hardware and home improvement stores. The gasket is achieved by covering the interior seam (of containers with side walls removed) with 1/4 in welded-on steel plate. This adds rigidity and acts as a support for the roofing cement as it is applied to the exterior gaps.

The top and side gaps should be filled with the roofing cement and allowed to set. Later, additional roofing cement and flashing can be applied to the top to form a water run-off channel and diversion spouts at each end of the structure.

6. Fitting Out Container Buildings

Fitting-out or "outfitting" containers describes all the aspects of building after initial placement on footings. These are projects such as cutting steel and installing doors and windows, insulation, wiring and so forth. You can build walls inside to create rooms, run wiring or plumbing, you could even install a hot-tub.

Many container builders simply build work benches and shelving inside for utility use. This is a very broad area of the building process which can be interpreted in many different ways.

Most of you will have a unique plan of out-fitting your building for your own specific use. Due to this fact I have included a sampling of ideas in this chapter that you can use as you see fit.

Cutting & Welding Container Steel

One of the major aspects of building with containers is working with steel. Many aspects of shipping container building requires cutting and removal of steel, and welding on components. Individuals not versed in welding should invest the time to learn proper techniques. Common methods for welding shipping container are: ARC/stick, MIG, TIG, or oxy-acetylene torch.

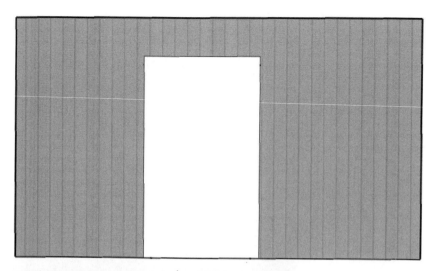

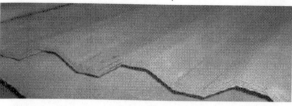

Left: sidewall panels are generally 14 gauge (.075" / 1.6mm-2.00mm) thick steel. The corrugated pattern is slightly more shallow than the end wall panel (as seen below).

Left: front end wall panel is (.075" / 1.6mm-2.00mm) thick steel. It makes up the far end opposite the door end. The door end is considered the rear of the unit due to it's placement on trucks facing the rear for loading etc.

You can cut the corrugated steel side panel materials with a oxy-acetylene torch, plasma torch, metal cutting band saw, nibbler, or a reciprocating saw with a metal blade. Wearing adequate safety gear like full face shield, welders apron, and gloves is recommended. Attempting to handle large segments of cut steel panels during removal is not advised as personal injury may result. The side wall panels, when cut in large segments, are deceivingly heavy. When removing a large segment of side wall panel it is best to cut smaller 2-4 foot wide sections out and remove each individually creating lighter easier handled pieces.

If preservation of a large piece of sidewall material is desired, say for use as a porch roof for example, adequate steps must be taken for support and safe removal when cutting. This is a engineering task unto itself that must be carefully planned. The most basic requirement for this is a large team of assistants for guiding the panel onto a forklift for removal. Holes may need to be created in the lower portion of the panel so as to allow forklift forks to enter, support, and lift out the panel. The holes can later be patched with sheet metal or the entire lower segment (with the holes) trimmed off.

Lumber can often safely be used as an alternative to many welded steel aspects presented here. Lumber for mid-span supports and door/window frames often costs less than structural steel. I will attempt to present both steel and wood options throughout this chapter.

The main production method for welding container corten steel is MIG with 80% argon, 20% CO2 gases.

Manual ARC stick welding is good for the small welding tasks involved in anchoring and fitting-out container buildings.

Oxy-acetylene torch welding can also be used for the thicker components of a container (corner fittings, rails, cross members, etc) but may warp side-wall material if used for window and doors frame angle stock.

MIG Solid Wire Sizes

(for use with standard 75% argon /25% CO2 shielding gas)

.030" wire (for up to .078" thick steel - side walls, roof panels, etc).

.035" wire (for .18" - .25" thick steel - side rails, structural angles, cross members, etc)

.045" wire (for .25" - .5" and up thick steel, corner fittings, foundation plates, anchoring, etc)

ARC (stick) Welding Electrodes

Arc (stick) welding electrodes (sticks) are made in sizes from 1/16 to 5/16

1/16" - 20-40amp (for welding up to 3/16" plate)

3/32" - 40-125amp (for welding up to 1/4" plate)

1/8" - 75-185amp (for welding over 1/8" plate)

5/32" - 105-250amp (for welding over 1/4" plate)

3/16" - 140-305amp (for welding over 3/8" plate)

1/4" - 210-430amp (for welding over 3/8" plate)

5/16" - 275-450amp (for welding over 1/2" plate)

ARC (stick) Welding Electrodes Types

E6011 This electrode is used for all position welding with AC and DC currents. It produces a deep penetrating weld and works well on dirty, rusted, or painted metals

E6013 This electrode can be used with AC and DC currents. It produces a medium penetrating weld with a superior weld bead appearance.

E7018 This is a low hydrogen electrode that can be used with AC or DC. It has a low moisture content coating that reduces the introduction of hydrogen into the weld. The electrode can produce high quality welds with medium penetration. Note: this electrode must be kept dry. If it gets wet, it must be dried in a rod oven before use.

Steel Stock

You will most likely want to purchase steel stock for certain structural aspects of your container building. Most general purpose steels fall under the category of 'mild steel'. Mild steel can be cut with oxy-acetylene torch, plasma torch, metal cutting band saw, nibbler, or a reciprocating saw with a metal blade.

When purchasing new steel stock for fabrication of container building, there are two main types you will commonly find depending on where you live. European buyers will utilize standard EN 10025 for steel that is described in a code beginning with the letter 'S' representing a structural steel (SXXXXX for example). Structural steels in the United States utilize ASTM International standards and always begin with the letter 'A' (A36 being the most commonly available example). A36 steel is a hot-rolled steel. It's the most common type of structural steel used in the United States.

Common variations of structural steel include: carbon steels, high strength low alloy steels, corrosion resistant high strength low alloy steels, quenched and tempered alloy steels, all of which vary in price and available shape. Generally, the stock shapes used for container fabrication include, but are not limited to: angle stock, plate, I-beam, round and square tube.

Salvaged steel can sometimes be used for fabricating certain aspects of a container building, but keep in mind the fact that it is usually sold to steel recyclers and not the general public, which is why you may not often find steel stock at a salvage yard. Steel doors, windows, and so forth can be found and adapted for use. Note: many salvage yards have liability policies in place the prohibit customers from picking out material themselves.

Also of interest are the recycled building material outlets now found in many areas. I have one near me. They sell a wide variety of used building materials, from doors to light fixtures.

Raw steel stock can be purchased in most urban areas from local steel vendors where you can choose from angle iron and plate steel in all shapes and sizes. Look under 'Steel Distributors & Warehouses' in the phone book to find these local outlets and inquire further about steel purchases.

Angle Stock

2" (A) x 2" (B) x 0.125" (C)

2" (A) x 2" (B) x 0.1875" (C)

2" (A) x 2" (B) x 0.25" (C)

2" (A) x 2" (B) x 0.375" (C)

2" (A) x 3" (B) x 0.1875" (C)

2" (A) x 3" (B) x 0.25" (C)

2.5" (A) x 2.5" (B) x 0.1875" (C)

2.5" (A) x 2.5" (B) x 0.25" (C)

2.5" (A) x 2.5" (B) x 0.375" (C)

3" (A) x 3" (B) x 0.1875" (C)

3" (A) x 3" (B) x 0.25" (C)

3" (A) x 3" (B) x 0.375" (C)

3" (A) x 3" (B) x 0.5" (C)

Commonly Available Steel Stock

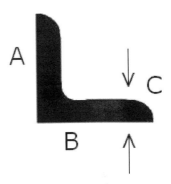

Square Tube

2" (A) x 0.12" (B)

2" (A) x 0.1875" (B)

2" (A) x 0.25" (B)

2.5" (A) x 0.12" (B)

2.5" (A) x 0.1875" (B)

2.5" (A) x 0.25" (B)

3" (A) x 0.12" (B)

3" (A) x 0.1875" (B)

3" (A) x 0.25" (B)

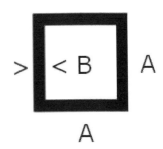

Steel stock can be used to fabricate door and window framing aspects. 2-3 in angle can be tack welded to side wall material forming a base to attach traditional framing lumber for installation of doors and windows.

Lumber can be screwed or bolted through holes pre-drilled in the angle material. The lands of the corrugated side wall material will weld flush to the (vertical planes) sides of the door opening.

The top angle, if placed correctly, will cover any gaps created by the corrugations. The trick is to weld the angle on from the outside of the container, allowing the leg (L) of the material to point in.

This also creates an attractive steel frame on the exterior that covers any imperfections in your door and window cut-outs -lumber alternative door and windows framing

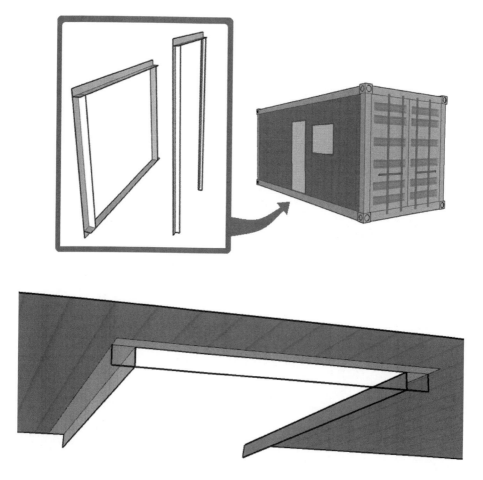

Angle stock is probably the most useful material for framing any cuts you make in a shipping container side walls.

Gaps are an obvious problem you will encounter during framing. These are a natural result of the peaks and valleys in the corrugated steel side panels. Roofing cement applied carefully using heavy masking tape works well and creates a clean line. You can also use expanding foam to fill gaps.

Several companies now produce a minimal expanding foam that provides a paintable surface and expands less offering greater control of application. Foam can be applied liberally and trimmed with a utility knife when dry.

Exterior and interior decorative trim can be used to cover unsightly cured foam.

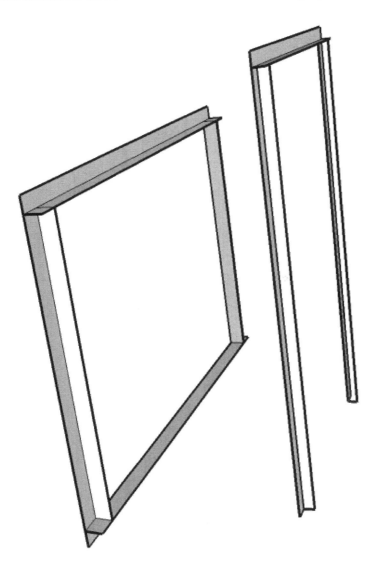

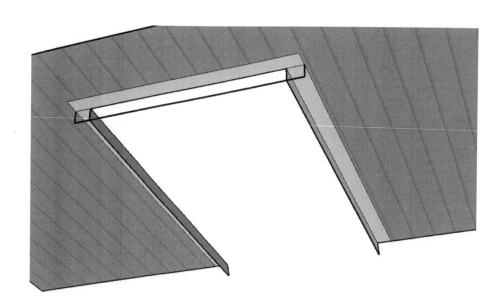

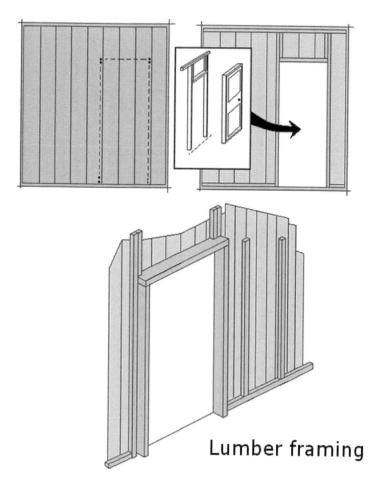

Lumber framing

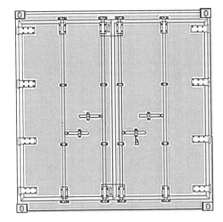
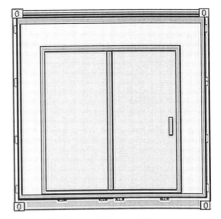

Sliding Glass Doors

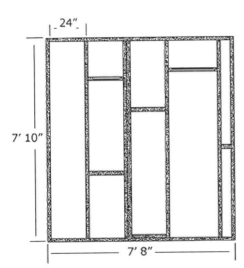

Replacement of open end steel cargo doors with a 2x4 framework and pre-hung door.

Optional: keep steel doors on unit, and install this framework set back 2 ft from opening.

This will create a dual door system: 1) daytime entry door, and 2) steel security doors that can be closed at night.

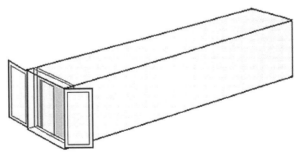

Decks are a natural extension of many container building layouts. The main thing to remember when planning a second level container deck is to keep the roof panels free from load bearing forces.

Container roof panels can only accept a 440 lb evenly distributed load (limited to a single 6 sq foot area at one time - like two people walking over it).

The load bearing aspects of second level decks should come to rest on the side rails as described in chapter five Roofing. Ground level decks can be anchored directly to the lower side rails.

The profiles below show some various ways in which a deck can be incorporated into your container structure.

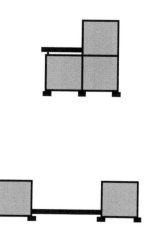

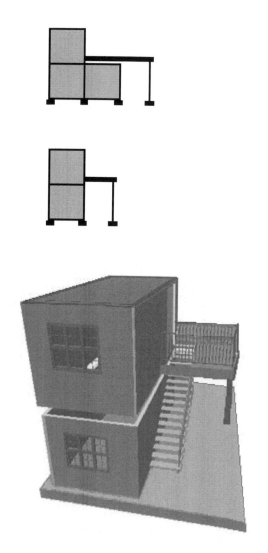

Stacking two containers and building a staircase to the second level doorway is a simple procedure for creating what in essence is a small apartment building.

Additional covered square footage can be obtained by expanding the deck.

Sliding glass doors can be installed in place of cargo doors.

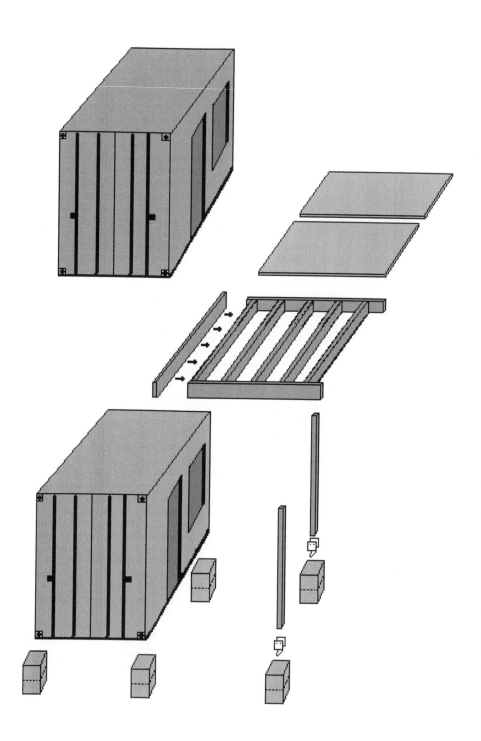

Insulating Container Buildings

If you live in a climate like I do (Puget Sound Washington), where the temperature does not fluctuate wildly, but rather remains in the 45-65F range most of the year, adding extraneous structural materials to combat climate is a not necessary.

Heating an un-insulated steel building in temps under 40F is not very cost effective and its almost impossible in temps under 20F. The same can be said for extreme summer heat.

Basic additional modifications for winter and summer container buildings are presented below. It's doubtful that this is a complete list of all possible methods, but it does offer a starting point and several usable options to combat climate.

Framing Interior

Since the container already possesses all of its load-bearing qualities built-in, strength of the framing material is not an issue. You can go as minimal as firing strips or 2x2s to mount paneling or insulating foam inside.

The easiest way to anchor framing components (studs) is to cut them precisely achieving a snug fit, then run a bead of Liquid Nails style construction adhesive on each stud, and tap it into place. Studs should be spaced 24 in on center to allow for easy attachment of 4x8 drywall or paneling materials.

This same method can be upgraded for cold weather buildings by using 2x4's or 2x6s and rolled fiberglass insulation.

Insulation Type	R-Value per inch	Materials	Use	Installation	Comments
Rolled Fiberglass	3.3	Glass fiber batts or blankets bundled in rolls	Lumber framed container walls, ceilings, and between cross members.	Fit between wood frame studs, joists, and beams.	Common, easy to install, and effective.
Rigid Panels	4.0 5.0 7.4 4.5	Molded polystyrene Extruded polystyrene Isocyanurate board Fiberglass board	Non-lumber framed container walls, ceilings, and between cross members.	Cut to fit and secure in place; should be covered with finishing material for fire safety.	High insulating value for relatively little thickness. Note: material can be flammable.

Flooring

Since the 1990's almost all standard containers have been manufactured with ply-wood floors. These floors are very strong and designed to support heavy pallets and loaded forklifts.

The panels used for these floors are commonly a 19-ply plywood product, approximately 1.10 inches (28 mm) thick, made from mixed hardwood species native to the Asian countries in which they are produced.

The plywood used in shipping container floors is usually treated to prevent infestation and rot. Exotic (possibly crop destroying) insects being brought into a country are a concern in global shipping, so containers are often fumigated.

This is not the rule, but some countries such as Australia are very stringent about it.

Older containers that don't have treated plywood floors usually have Teak floors. Teak is naturally resistant to insects, including termites. It's own natural oils are antiseptic and insects won't eat it. It has a natural UV protecting property.

If you are concerned about chemicals and crud in the flooring, you can cover the floor with a new layer of plywood, a vinyl roll type flooring, or an industrial carpet.

Total replacement of flooring is a difficult job but not impossible. Replacing damaged sections of plywood is a not unheard of practice in the shipping industry. If you notice some sections of your used container floor are newer than others, this is most likely what happened.

Some builders have covered the existing container floor with high grade hardwood flooring for a very finished look. This is a nice option if the unit will be used as residential or perhaps an art gallery or retail store.

Painting Containers

Even if you do not plan to paint an entire container, stripped/welded areas will require touching up. The process of painting lends itself to both full refurbishment and touch up tasks.

a) Surface preparation; all dirt, moisture, oil, grease, loose rust and impurities must be removed. For small areas, grinding discs, wire brushes, and solvent can be used. For large areas, abrasive blasting is required. Compressed air can be used to remove dust and dry solvents in both cases.

b) Selecting paint; the primer you use should be chemically compatible with the existing old paint. Check the interior of the container, on the right side near the door, for markings indicating the original top coat. Corten steel does not require zinc-rich epoxy primers since it already possesses it's anit-corrosive qualities. Information about the original paint may not be available. If this is the case, use a high quality primer and top coat for steel.

Factory Container Preservation

Steel Surface Preparation

a) Steel is degreased and shot blasted to a surface roughness of 25 to 35 microns removing all rust, dirt, mill scale and all other foreign materials.
b) The floor panels, all interior joints, and all bolt holes are sealed to prevent water entry.

Sealant Materials:
a. Chloroprene (Cargo contact area)
b. Butyl (Hidden parts)

Paint Specifications

Prior to Assembly
All steel surfaces are coated with a primer paint immediately after shot-blasting.

Paint
Exterior Surface: epoxy zinc rich primer, epoxy primer, acrylic top coat
Interior Surface: epoxy zinc rich primer, epoxy top coat
Under Structure: epoxy zinc rich primer, waxy bitumen

South Korean Hanjin Intermodal facility at Pier 46 in Seattle

Container ship from China is unloaded at Pier 46 in Seattle

Inbound container ship is dwarfed by 14,410 foot Mt. Rainier

Hong Kong marked container ship arrives at Pier 46 in Seattle

Shipping containers are stacked seven high on deck

Surplus containers for sale off the I5 corridor Seattle Tacoma

Containers for sale near Seattle

Containers at a Grand Trunk Western Railroad yard near Detroit

95

7. Three Minimal Modification Designs

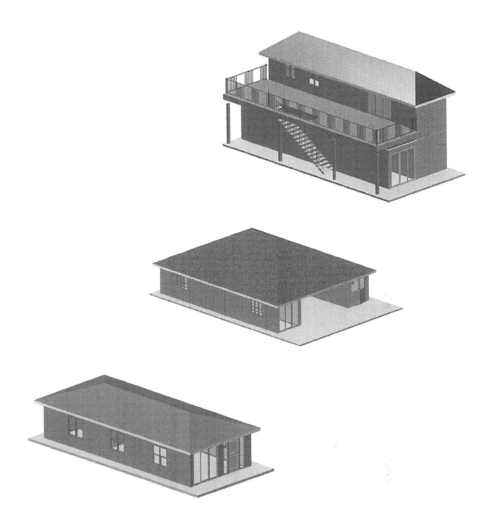

This section contains images of what I feel are the three best plans for container buildings under 1000 sq ft in size. I call these the best plans simply because they offer good solutions for the major needs of most small steel building users.

These structures can be fitted out for a variety of uses, ranging from utility to residential. They can be built quickly and for less money than comparable lumber or factory steel buildings.

The following pages contain drawings and some discussion of these plans. Detailed blueprints with extensive dimensions are not included because, as we know, container dimensions are fixed to ISO standard 668. Dimensional and structural unknowns certainly exist, but these are best calculated by the individual builder when developing his or her own unique design.

Most people who want to setup any sort of building without the use of hired help will spend a considerable amount of time in the planning stage. This is the time when some lofty ideas are often dismissed as too difficult or expensive. This 'weeding out' process is a natural progression from original idea to a realistic design many will experience.

Some simple building plans can be offered to the would-be builder who is open to using a basic design to further his or her real pursuit of art, welding, fabrication, repair, etc. These are the users of the structures aptly named in the title of this book 'small steel buildings'.

To many, the structure is just a tool to further a main interest in some other form of art or craftsmanship. Sometimes its just a place to store stuff, or a 'fortress' for spending free time doing whatever the builder pleases.

Whatever the case, many are satisfied with just a solid foundation, four walls, and some sort of roof. The building itself need not convey impressive architectural aspects, but if this occurs as a side effect so be it.

With all this in mind I present what I feel are the top three 'minimal modification' designs. Below is a bullet point list of what these designs all have in common from a construction and planning point of view.

° The containers should receive minimal removal of side-wall material. This insures that a good portion of the containers original specified rigidity remains intact reducing the wild card engineering aspects that often occur with side-wall removal.

° Multi level designs utilize corner-post-to-corner-post placement taking advantage of containers built-in stackable nature. Again, this reduces any chance of unexpected engineering problems as a result of unnatural stresses placed on the side rails.

° Pre-planned and poured concrete footing or slab components are built far in advance of container arrival allowing proper cure time.

° Rapid roughed-in construction by way of one day container placement with additional structural aspects built on a relaxed schedule when time and money permits.

Basic Outline of the Container Building Process

Step 1: Build concrete foundation aspects one month prior to container delivery and placement.

Step 2: Take delivery of containers, place containers onto foundation slab or footings by way of crane rental. Check and adjust square and level of placement.

Step 3: Anchor containers together with clamps, bolts, welded steel plates.

Step 4: Remove side wall material, and seal seam of joined units (if required).

Step 5: Install top plates for roof (if required).

Step 6: Measure and cut studs for rafter or truss roof construction (if required).

Step 7: Install roof frame system (if required).

Step 8: Sheath roof and install final roofing materials (if required).

Step 9: Measure and cut steel (make sure to double check all aspects before making any cuts) for doors, and windows.

Step 10: Install interior framing, windows, and pre-hung doors.

Step 11: Complete the fitting out of your building by painting, and installing interior elements, and utilities.

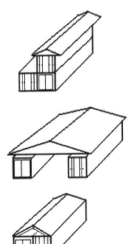

Design Name	Possible Uses
Triple 40	Office over shop. Residence.
Super Carport	Car, motorcycle, RV, boat, storage or repair facility. Dual office with covered outdoor lounge area. Pool house, or covered hot tub sauna structure.
Side-by- Side	Utility, storage, repair facility. Classroom or office. Residence.

Triple 40

When you build a structure with three 40 foot shipping containers using the 'Triple 40' design, you are creating a side-by-side ground level structure with a third single unit placed on top. The nice thing about this design it how easily it adapts to the addition of a second floor sun deck or covered porch. Such decking aspects should be built by placing load bearing beams on corner fittings, thus transferring stresses down the corner posts and avoiding contact with the roof panels.

Bottom floor containers should keep full side walls intact for maximum strength in support of the upper level unit. Upper level containers can receive some minor side wall removal for installation of a sliding glass door and so forth.

Super Carport

The 'Super Carport' is a great design that perhaps suffers from one 'catch 22'. While it offers a container based structure with a scaleable wide open inside space, it does require additional expenditures and labor for the roofing aspects. To many this is not a big deal, and well worth it to create a large covered structure with lockable shipping container units at each end for additional stowage.

This type of container building is ideal for vehicle and boat storage because it can be custom built to fit the vehicle or boat you have. You can construct a single level carport using standard height containers on each end, or a slightly higher single level carport using high cube containers. Similarly, a two level carport can be built from standard or high cube shipping containers. This offers four possible heights of covered structure to accommodate various size vehicles or boats.

° **Single level (standard height container) carport = 8.5 foot ceiling height**

° **Single level (high cube container) carport = 9.5 foot ceiling height**

° **Two level (standard height container) carport = 17 foot ceiling height**

° **Two level (high cube container) carport = 19 foot ceiling height**

Side-by-Side

This is the classic 'one up' from a single container in design terms. It's not a complicated design, but it does offer the ability to create somewhat of a larger inside space by way of some side wall removal. Placing two containers in a side-by-side layout also opens up the possibility of future expansion of the structure, by placing additional units on the sides or by stacking more on top. Avoid stacking containers over the side-by-side building that has received substantial side wall removal as it will likely lack the required rigidity to properly support a second unit placed on top.

Triple 40

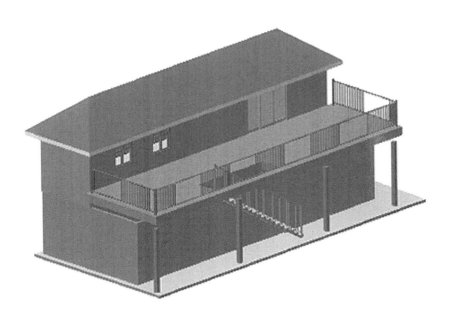

Super Carport

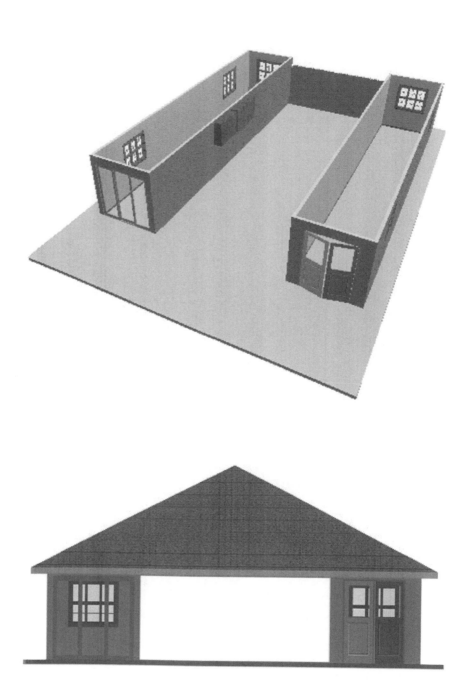

Side-by-Side

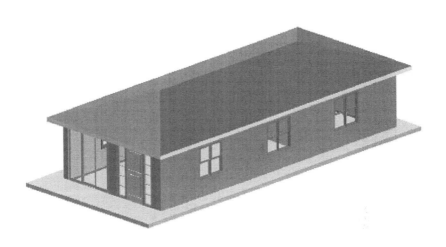

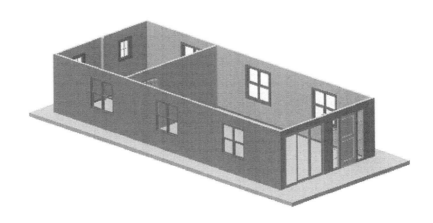

8. Miscellaneous Container Building Ideas

Mini Triple

Three 20 ft containers. Smaller 20 foot variation of The Triple 40. Useful as a multi-level cabin, cottage, or guest house.

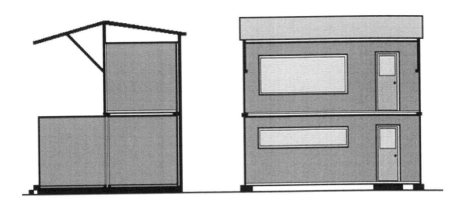

Sports Building

Two 20 ft stacked containers. Could be used for sporting events, announcers booth, concessions stand, or equipment storage. Possible applications: high schools, skeet and trap clubs, dirt-bike, horse, or dog racing facilities.

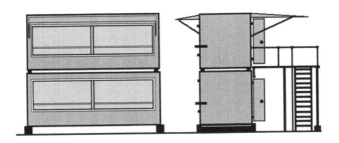

Ranch House

Two 40 ft containers, and one 20 ft container. The single 20 ft unit is bridged across the end of two parallel 40 ft units to form a horseshoe shaped, three room building with a rafter built roof.

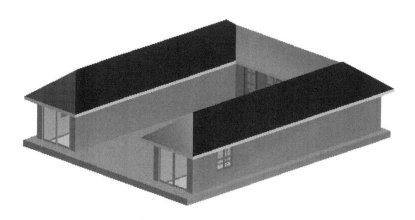

Split Level

One 40 ft container, with an additional one, or two 20 ft containers stacked on top. Upper level 20 ft containers are braced at the midway point with a steel I-beam suspension system. This transfers the weight of the second, and optional third floors to the ground, bypassing the (non load bearing) center of the 40 ft base unit.

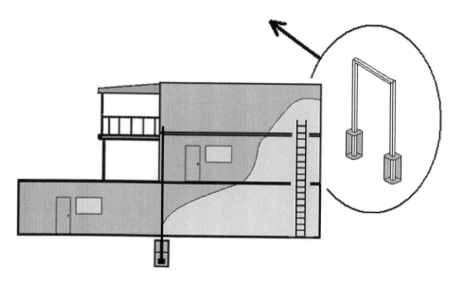

Flood Proof

A single 20 ft x 8.5 ft container is attached to a steel I-beam framework foundation (container can be raised 6-12 ft above ground level using this system). May be useful in deep snow, flood or tsunami prone regions. Four vertical I-beams are sunk into underground (2 ft x 3 ft concrete) footings providing a high strength foundation for container mounting.

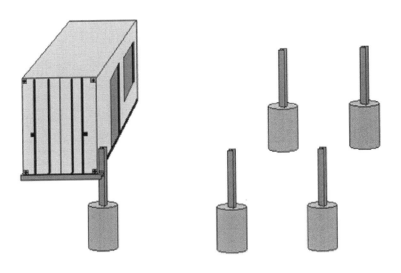

Solar Cabin

One 20 ft container with modernistic steel roof and solar panels. Roof shades the container from hot sun, while simultaneously generating all required electrical power for the occupant. Another option is to replace cargo doors with a 6' glass patio slider, or install a glass patio slider behind the cargo doors for a dual-use door system.

Cube

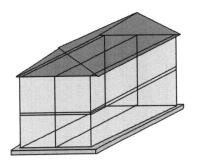

Four 20 ft containers joined, and stacked to form a cube. Building is set on concrete footings, and covered with a gable roof.

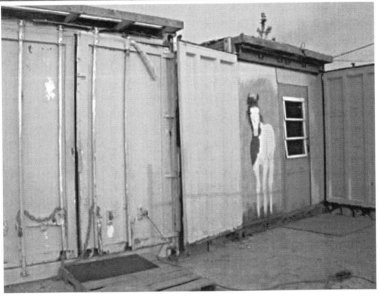

Arkwild, Inc, (www.arkwild.org) and its offshoot WHOA, Wild Horses of Abaco Preservation Society, is using two 20 ft containers to raise funds for a herd of rare horses on Abaco Island in the Bahamas. One container is an office, the other a book shop with assorted media exchanged for donations.

One container was placed with a forklift, the second with a crane. The boxes are directly on blacktop. Both box roofs were tarred and papered to stop leaks. They were insulated on the outside, the insulation fastened with battens in anticipation of adding siding.

The arrival of two hurricanes in Sept. and Oct. of 2004 blew away most of the insulation with gusts up to at least 150 miles an hour and in the second storm floods put 9" of water in both containers.

As a pre storm precaution half inch chain tied the bases of the containers together and lengths of chain connected both containers to chain link fence posts sunk in concrete.

The containers did not move even though during the second storm they were hit broad side (on both sides) due to the eye going right over the area.

"As a charity we cannot afford rent, nor can we afford to build anything. The containers have been safe, strong and secure. It is hoped that at some point we can replace the insulation, apply siding and do some landscaping to bring them up to their full potential visually. They are invaluable to the project." Arkwild

Special Thanks to Arkwild, Inc, (www.arkwild.org)

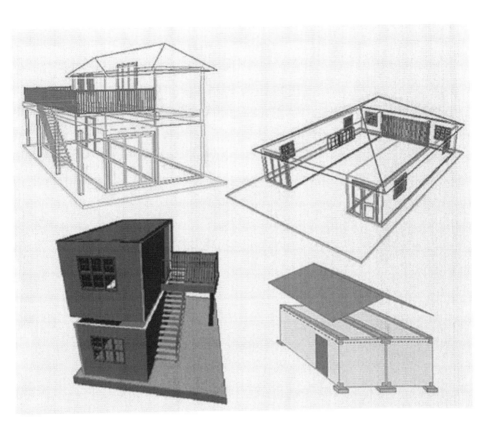

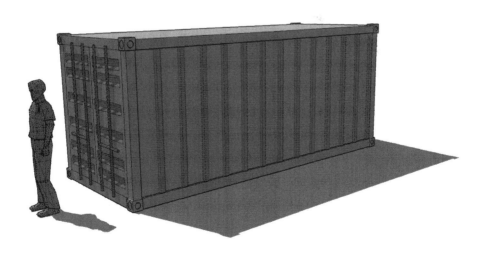

References

Intermodal Association of North America (IANA), Intermodal.org

Journal of Commerce PIERS - Port Import/Export Reporting Service

Shipping Statistics Yearbook 2005

Containerisation International Yearbook 2006

American Association of Port Authorities (AAPA) Advisory, 2006

GVD Container Handbook

Fabrication and Erection of Structural Steel for Buildings, American Institute of Steel Construction, 1978

Containerbay, Fabprefab.com, and the various websites featured

Guide to Container Inspection for Commercial and Military Intermodal Containers, MIL-HDBK-138B, 2002, US

Online Metals - Guide to Buying Steel Online, onlinemetals.com

Institute of International Container Lessors, IICL, Repair Manual for Steel Freight Containers (fifth edition)

Technical Specifications for 40ft, 40ft highcube, 20ft, 20ft highcube, Steel Dry Cargo Containers, 2007

American National Standards Institute various ISO standards

This book was produced and distributed by

PAUL SAWYERS PUBLICATIONS

WWW.PAULSAWYERS.COM

Made in the USA
San Bernardino, CA
21 December 2014